C000194807

SURPLUS PEOPLE
FROM WICKLOW TO CANADA

JIM REES, a Wicklow resident and historian, with a History Masters Degree from NUI Maynooth, has had a lifelong passion for history and literature. He has written extensively and lectured widely on topics such as emigration and maritime history.

Keep up to date with Jim Rees on Facebook at www.facebook.com/jim.rees.391?fref=ts

SURPLUS PEOPLE
FROM WICKLOW TO CANADA

JIM REES

The Collins Press

PUBLISHED IN 2014 BY
The Collins Press
West Link Park
Doughcloyne
Wilton
Cork

First published in 2000

A CIP record for this book is available from the British Library.

Paperback ISBN: 978-1-84889-204-0
PDF eBook ISBN: 978-1-84889-850-9
EPUB eBook ISBN: 978-1-84889-851-6
Kindle ISBN: 978-1-84889-852-3

Typesetting by The Collins Press
Typeset in Palatino

Printed in Malta by Gutenberg Press Ltd

CONTENTS

PICTURE CREDITS

The publishers and author would like to thank all who have supplied illustrations for this book.

Page 10: Trustees of the Right Honourable Olive, Countess Fitzwilliam's Chattels Settlement and Lady Juliet de Chair.
Page 14: William Nolan, Geography Publications.
Pages 45, 48, 50, 52, 54: *Illustrated London News*.
Pages 60, 62, 72, 74: André Charbonneau, Parcs Canada.
Page 84: Robbie Tyrrell.
Page 143: The outboard sketch of the barque *Dunbrody*, © Colin Mudie.

Acknowledgements

I began researching this book in 1995 and it took about three years to complete. I was fortunate to receive the help and goodwill of many people during that time. I wish to thank the Director and staff of the National Library of Ireland; Brian Donnelly and Ken Hannigan of the National Archives of Ireland; Billy Lee, John Murphy, Joe Hayden, the late Paudge Brennan, Pat Power, Mary Kelly Quinn, and Richard Haworth. Mary Byrne deciphered many of the documents and put them on computer.

I must mention the generous help and co-operation of Denis Noel of the Provincial Archives of New Brunswick, Allen Doiron also of the PANB, Mary McDevitt the Archivist of the Diocese of St John, Professor Gail Campbell of St Thomas' University, George Haney, Joan Jones, Anne Brault, Hilarion and Patricia Coughlin, and all the members of the Irish Canadian Cultural Association who helped in so many ways. I must thank Marianna O'Gallagher in Quebec and Tom and Mary-Anne Birchard, Kyle, Meghan, and Garrett in Toronto. Among my informants were descendants of some of the emigrants whose story is recorded here. I am particularly grateful to Ron Brash, Paul Ormond, Terri Brickett, Marian Gamester, Bob Beckwith and Gail Nightingale. Both Lois Long of Ottawa and Ross Hopkins of Rossland, BC, deserve very special mention for supplying me not only with information about their ancestors but also for sharing the fruits of their very extensive researches.

Without financial support, I could not have undertaken research in Canada. In this regard special thanks are due to the O'Mahony family who provided research funding through the EOIN O'MAHONY BURSARY, which is administered by the Royal Irish Academy.

CURRENCY CONVERSION

Below is a table of modern equivalents of the main contemporary monetary amounts mentioned in the text. Finding an appropriate indicator to compare relative worth is a complex business, as there are many and varied methods from which to choose, and the result is, of necessity, merely an approximation. I have used a comparison of average earnings as the basis, from the website MeasuringWorth.com.

1847–1856	2010s
Five shillings	€200
Ten shillings	€400
£3-15-0	€3,000
£5	€4,000
£10-15-0	€9,000
£20	€17,000
£40-5-6	€33,000
£3,000	€2.6 million
£16,342-11-1	€14 million
£24,000	€20 million

INTRODUCTION

The Irish potato famine of the second half of the 1840s was a catastrophe of immense proportions. It has been described as the worst social disaster of nineteenth-century Europe. Its scale was so vast that historians disagree on many of its aspects. How many died, how many emigrated, how much or how little was done by government to alleviate the suffering of millions; how great was its social and cultural impact? Was it famine or simply a series of crop failures? Was it the will of God or passive genocide? They cannot even agree on how long it lasted. Its duration is difficult to define because it did not 'end' but rather petered out, with some regions experiencing crop failures for seven consecutive years from 1845 to 1852.[1]

So much has been written about that horrific time that it is sometimes tempting to think that there are no new angles from which to view it. That would be a great mistake. As historians dig deeper, new facts leading to new interpretations come to light. Also, when an event of such magnitude is looked at on a national level, the overall picture can only be brought into focus at the loss of localised detail. The potato crop failures of those years varied in intensity and geographical distribution and there has been an understandable tendency to concentrate on those areas which were hardest hit. Because of this tendency many parts of the country have been overlooked or, at best, only briefly referred to.

One of those regions is County Wicklow which, in common with most of the eastern counties, figures scantily, if at all, in most of the major studies. This meagre coverage is unintentionally misleading and perpetuates the misconception that Wicklow somehow managed to come through those years unscathed.

Recent studies have shown that death from starvation and

disease in Wicklow was more common than had been realised.[2] The Workhouses in Shillelagh, Rathdrum, Baltinglass and Rathdown were filled to overflowing. Government schemes, soup kitchens and local relief committees operated throughout the county. Eviction and emigration were also part of Wicklow's famine experience. It has been estimated that the population of the county decreased by 21.5% between 1841 and 1851. This decrease represented over 27,000 people. The proximity of the national capital offered an escape route for many and by 1851 'more than a fifth of all Wicklow-born people lived in Dublin'.[3] There were also many thousands who went to Britain, the United States and Canada. In 1850, the parish priest of the combined parish of Killaveny and Annacurra, in the south of the county, led over a thousand people to the American mid-west at the behest of the Bishop of Little Rock in Arkansas.[4]

Landlords, eager to rid their estates of 'surplus' tenantry, were engaged in 'assisted passages'. The most important of these was Lord Fitzwilliam, whose 80,000-acre estate was by far the largest in the county. Between 1847 and 1856 he removed almost 6,000 men, women and children from his property and arranged passage for them to Canada. Most of them were destitute and arrived in Quebec and New Brunswick with little more than what they wore on their backs.

The purpose of this study is to examine the Fitzwilliam clearances during those years and, where possible, to see how some of the families fared on their arrival in Canada. It will be noticed that while a complete chapter is dedicated to the situation on the infamous Grosse Île near Quebec, there is little information in this work about how these families fared when they reached their destinations in Ontario and elsewhere. This was due to time and financial restrictions during the research period. However, I have included a detailed chapter dealing with those families who arrived in St Andrews, New Brunswick.

Chapter 1

COOLATTIN ESTATE

Coolattin is synonymous with the Fitzwilliam family, who owned the property for 200 years before selling it in the 1970s.

The district in which the Coolattin estate lay was once part of the lands controlled by the native Irish sept of the O'Byrnes. Although there is evidence to show that the Normans made some attempt to settle the area, it was not until the sixteenth century that English influence was eventually felt. In 1578, Sir Henry Harrington, an adventurer, was granted the 'country of Shilelaughe alias Shilealie in County Dublin,[1] lying nigh the Birenes country, in the queen's disposition as by good matter of record doth appear. To hold for twenty-one years, rent £13-6-8'.[2]

This was hostile country for people like Harrington and one of the stipulations of the lease was that he had to maintain a corps of English horsemen. The indigenous inhabitants were, understandably, sometimes less than compliant with leases that had been drawn up without their consultation. Harrington immediately set about building a stone castle in the townland of Knockloe. It did little to deter the O'Byrnes from registering their displeasure at his intrusion and they razed it in a subsequent battle in 1597. Equally undeterred, Harrington built another castle a few years later at Carnew. This one withstood the test of time and tumult and a substantial portion of it, incorporated into a more recent building, can still be seen in the village.

When Harrington died in 1612 his property passed into the hands of a Welshman, Calcott Chambre. By this time, the O'Byrnes had submitted to English rule and the county of Wicklow had come into being, the last of the 32 counties in Ireland to be established. This led to a period of uneasy peace. Free from the restrictions of defence requirements, Chambre established a deer park encompassing about seven miles around the castle but his main interest was in smelting iron ore. The vast woodlands in the area offered long-term sources of fuel with which to extract the metal from the ore, which was then imported as pig iron from Wales. So plentiful and cheaply obtainable was the timber fuel that the ore could be brought from Wales, smelted and exported back across the Irish Sea and still be sold more profitably than if it were produced in Wales or England.

Chambre was not the only entrepreneur to seize upon this opportunity. There were small smelters operating in clusters throughout what was to become the Coolattin estate. In general, the people who worked them were non-native and transient, without ties to the land or the area, who were here simply to smelt ore while the cheap fuel supply lasted. Chambre, however, was by far the most successful.

THE EARL OF STRAFFORD

Thomas Wentworth, 1st Earl of Strafford, was a remarkable entrepreneur. He was ambitious, shrewd, clever, conniving, manipulative and scheming. In the 1630s, he was appointed Lord Deputy of Ireland, in effect the king's representative, a viceroy with immense power and endless opportunity to increase his already considerable fortune. He quickly established a reputation for implementing his own agenda without regard for others and consequently earned the name 'Black Tom'.

Wentworth, despite having property in Yorkshire and

Northamptonshire, wanted to establish himself firmly in Ireland and in a seven year period he acquired 60,000 acres in County Wicklow. Some of this property he acquired in 1638 from Calcott Chambre. When he first approached Chambre with a view to buying him out, Chambre was not interested. However, as Lord Deputy, Wentworth had the power to impose or relax trading restrictions at will and he consequently introduced an export tax on smelted iron. This, of course, greatly curtailed Chambre's business yet he still refused to sell to Wentworth. Black Tom was equally determined that the sale should go ahead and he had Chambre arrested and imprisoned. Chambre eventually conceded and Wentworth bought the land around Shillelagh, paying £13,000 for 24,000 acres. Shortly afterwards, he acquired the manors of Wicklow and Newcastle as well as lands in the Towerboy and Cashaw areas of the county.

Since Wentworth was, first and foremost, the king's man, Charles I supported Wentworth when his enemies bayed for his blood, as long as there was no great threat to himself. By 1640, however, the baying became so pronounced that Wentworth was becoming more of a problem than a prop. In May of the following year, to appease the growing anti-Wentworth lobby, Charles agreed to have 'his man' executed at Tyburn. The charges which led to Wentworth's beheading branded him a traitor and the sentence called for, apart from his death, confiscation of his lands by the Crown.

That should have been the end of the Wentworth wealth but politics is a strange game in which the rules continually change, and before the year was out the properties were restored to Wentworth's son, the 2nd Earl of Strafford. This was the beginning of the see-saw claims of the Wentworths to their Shillelagh properties, which they referred to as Fairwood. Within two years of regaining the lands from the Crown, the properties were again confiscated by those in power. This time, civil war in England raged between Royalists and Cromwell's Roundheads. In 1643, the Roundheads held sway and they stripped known Royalists of their possessions. Consequently the Wentworths lost their lands because, firstly, they were deemed anti-royalist and, secondly, because they were deemed pro-royalist. The eventual disillusion with Cromwell's Commonwealth and the restoration of the monarchy in 1660 once again reversed the fortunes of the Wentworths and they regained their estates and titles. By 1663, all was almost as it had been in Black Tom's day.

Whereas Tom had planned on investing heavily in his Wicklow properties, his son showed no interest in them, as long as the felling of the woods produced the revenue he had come to expect from them. In fact, it is doubtful if he ever even visited Ireland. When he died in 1695, at the age of 69, he had no children to inherit either the Fairwood estate or his vast properties in England. The main estate was at Wentworth-Woodhouse in Yorkshire. The person with the greatest claim to the properties was 30-year-old Thomas Watson, the third son of Wentworth's eldest sister who was married to Edward Watson, the 2nd Baron Rockingham.[3]

THE MARQUIS OF ROCKINGHAM

A codicil of Thomas Wentworth's will was that his successor must adopt the name Wentworth. When Thomas Watson inherited the Strafford properties, therefore, he changed his name to Thomas Watson-Wentworth.

Like his benefactor, Thomas never came to Ireland. As long as it produced a steady income and did not impinge too deeply on his time, he was happy to let life at Fairwood proceed as it had done. He was more concerned with his properties and prospects in England. In 1728 he became Baron Malton, becoming the Earl of Malton ten years later and it was at about this time the

4

name of his Shillelagh estate changed from Fairwood to Malton, and he set about taking an active interest in his Irish estate.

The political uncertainties of the latter half of the seventeenth century made investment in Irish properties a particularly precarious prospect. However, the establishment of a Protestant monarchy, aristocracy, and administration, the imposition of the Penal Laws against Catholics and non-conformists, and other factors helped stabilise the economy. Also, decades of forestry clearance with no thought of long-term replacement meant that the only source of revenue was beginning to disappear. A complete reversal of attitude towards the Fairwood/Malton estate was called for.

As the fortunes of the estate, or the lack of them, were being assessed, the strength of the tenants' hold on the lands was recognised for the first time. In the asset-stripping mindset which had prevailed the tenants had been ignored. This suited the tenants as their rents were, on average, half of what tenants on other estates, particularly in neighbouring County Wexford, were paying to their landlords for comparative holdings. Also, they had managed to secure leases which incorporated the 'Ulster Custom'. This allowed the tenant to nominate the holder of the new lease on the expiration of the current one. He could even name himself. In effect, this gave the tenants indefinite tenure. The rents could be raised with each new lease but it would be up to the tenant if he wished to renew it or pass it on to a son or other designate. Also, the size of their holdings were very large. In 1730, out of a population in excess of 5,000 people on the Fairwood/Malton estate, there were only 64 head-tenants and these, left to their own devices for so long, wielded more power on the estate than either Wentworth or Thomas Watson-Wentworth.

Their houses and lifestyle reflected this independence and power. Hugh Wainwright, Watson-Wentworth's agent on

the estate and the man charged with implementing the policy
changes to make it profitable, complained that the houses of the
head-tenants were too large to be maintained by their holdings.
Meanwhile, their sub-tenants were living in wretched hovels. If
the estate was to be turned around the grip of the head-tenants
would have to be broken. With the final suppression of the
Jacobite cause in 1745–6, even greater and more prolonged
stability was assured and the time had come to implement the
new policies to the full. Even better was the fact that in 1746
Thomas Watson-Wentworth inherited the vast Rockingham
estates from the paternal side of his family. He was now the
Marquis of Rockingham, with the combined fortunes of the
Rockinghams and the Wentworths behind him.

From that time, new clauses in leases were introduced as
they came up for renewal. Rents were raised and the first
wisps of change could be felt. But in 1750, before the new
measures could be fully introduced, Thomas Watson-
Wentworth died.

While Watson-Wentworth's material fortunes had grown,
he had been less blessed in his family life. His first four sons
pre-deceased him, so it was his fifth son, Charles, who became
the 2nd Marquis of Rockingham. Charles had established a
reputation as something of a radical. He was one of the leading
proponents of Catholic Emancipation and he was a supporter
of the efforts to establish a parliament in Dublin which would
deal with internal Irish matters, although still subject to the
English parliament when it came to foreign affairs and defence.
Unfortunately, when this demi-parliament was opened in 1782
it proved to be nothing more than a Protestant assembly for a
Protestant, propertied elite. The majority of the people of
Ireland had no representation in it.

This was the man who turned the estate around. Before new
leases were signed, the tenants had to accept certain conditions
– trees were to be planted, fences made, and cottage industries

were to be introduced. Each tenant was to produce a certain quantity of linen each year. The growing of flax and the resultant linen industry had worked very well in Ulster and, he felt, might well be replicated in Wicklow. Such plans seldom make allowance for local conditions and what seemed a good idea proved unworkable, although some linen manufacture did take place for a couple of decades. But the greatest social change on the estate wrought in his years was the dramatic loss of power of the head-tenants. In 1745, 4% of tenants had holdings of less than 60 acres while 40% had from 300 to 1,000 acres. By 1783, 41% had holdings of less than 60 acres while the percentage of 300- to 1,000-acre tenants had tumbled from 40% to 13%. He had broken the hold of the middlemen to a large degree. While this was of immense importance to the estate, it mattered little to the sub-tenants in the hovels.

Like the last of the Straffords, Charles also died without an heir and, once again, a near relative was sought who would have a legal claim to the properties in both England and Ireland. Charles had three sisters, the eldest of whom, Anne, had married the 3rd Earl Fitzwilliam in 1744. Fitzwilliam had died in 1756, leaving her a widow with an eight-year-old son, William. William became the 4th Earl Fitzwilliam and was the incumbent of the title when his maternal uncle, Charles Watson-Wentworth, the 2nd Marquis of Rockingham, died in 1782 leaving him the vast fortune which included the Malton estate based at Shillelagh.

THE FITZWILLIAMS

The Fitzwilliams had long been established in England and, over the centuries, had held some very important posts. One had been the Lord Lieutenant of Ireland for almost 30 years in the sixteenth century. They were also connected by marriage to many of England's most prosperous and powerful families including the Duke of Devonshire and the Earls of Liverpool and Leicester. They were staunch royalists and were close to the throne. Their ability to shift with the prevailing political winds assured them of success and security of tenure. As in many cases, their conversion to Protestantism during the Reformation was generally considered to have been based on economics rather than sincerity and their ambiguous attitudes towards Catholicism caused frequent suspicion, if not open accusation. It was a trait that was to manifest itself time and again.

The 4th Earl, who inherited Malton estate as part of the Rockingham legacy, was a remarkable character. He was described in Rosebery's *Life of Pitt* as: '... a man of courageous sympathies and honest enthusiasm, but not less wrongheaded as strongheaded, absolutely devoid of judgement, reticence, and tact.'

This unflattering assessment stemmed from Fitzwilliam's period as Lord Lieutenant of Ireland shortly before the outbreak of the 1798 Rebellion. Unlike his ancestor of the sixteenth century who had held the post for three decades, this Fitzwilliam held the position for a mere eight months. In fact, he was in Dublin only from December 1794 to March 1795, just 80 days, before being recalled to London. His well known and frankly proclaimed sympathies with Catholic Emancipation were not welcomed by the Irish parliament. He believed that religious bigotry was not only morally wrong but economically unwise. Nor did he restrict his support of religious freedom to inopportune utterances. He donated land and money to have Catholic churches erected on his estate at a time when many landlords would not even give permission for such building let alone contribute to its cost.[4]

His sympathies for the oppressed were not restricted to Irish Catholics. More than twenty years after his removal as Lord Lieutenant for Ireland, he became embroiled in the rights of the English poor. In 1819, a large meeting was held at St Peter's Field in Manchester to urge parliamentary reform to alleviate the dire distress of the poor in England. The standard of living had deteriorated greatly in the depression following the Napoleonic Wars. In time-honoured fashion, parliament, rather than addressing the issue, sent in troops who attacked the assembly, killing eleven. There was an outcry against this event which became known as the Peterloo Massacre. Fitzwilliam was quick to add his voice in protest with the result that he was removed from the post of Lord Lieutenant of the West Riding of Yorkshire, a position he had held since leaving Ireland in 1798.

He had been 34 years old when he succeeded to the Malton estate, which he renamed Coolattin, and he continued the policies of new tenancy agreements which were, by now, well established. This, along with his support of Catholic Emancipation and other radical views, caused a great deal of ill-will between him and the head-tenants. For decades they had seen their power eroded. Their social standing and their economic base had been systematically chipped away. Little wonder that in the months before open rebellion broke out in May 1798, the Carnew, Shillelagh, and Tinahely yeoman militias, which were made up of head-tenants and other middle-class Protestants on the Coolattin estate, were among the most ferocious in their dealings with Catholic neighbours. Likewise, the first Orange Lodge in the county was established at Tinahely. This consolidation of middle-class Protestant interests was a direct result of the erosion of the position which their grandfathers had established. Distrust and division between the estate and head-tenants, and head-tenants and sub-tenants became the order of the day. These social scars were a long time in healing and, even now, traces can still be detected.

It will be remembered that, as a condition of inheriting the

Charles, 5th Earl of Fitzwilliam, at the age of sixteen

Strafford estates in 1695, Thomas Watson incorporated the name Wentworth into his own. In 1807, Fitzwilliam did precisely the same thing and by royal licence became William Wentworth-Fitzwilliam. This apparent continuity of surname helped create the image of unbroken ownership of the properties.

In 1823, at the age of 75, Fitzwilliam married for the second time. His bride was Louise, the 73-year-old widow of Baron Ponsonby. She died fourteen months later but the earl survived her by another eight years, dying in 1833.[5]

As with the Straffords, the Rockinghams and the rest of the aristocracy, the Fitzwilliams had as many titles as a well-stocked bookshop. One of these was Lord Milton and this was bestowed on the heir apparent to the main title of Earl Fitzwilliam. Until the 4th Earl died, his eldest son Charles William was Lord Milton. Charles had been born in 1786 and was imbued with the liberal attitudes of his father. He entered parliament at the age of twenty and from 1806 to 1833 was Whig MP for various constituencies. He espoused the cause of wider suffrage and was particularly vociferous in the early 1830s when the Reform Bill was introduced to parliament. This was a time of unprecedented social unrest in Britain. The economy was in tatters and those who bore the brunt were the poor. Many social and parliamentary changes were urged to defuse the situation which increasingly threatened upheaval. Among these reforms was the liberalisation of representation in the House of Commons. The Whigs proposed to enfranchise large industrial towns which had not previously been represented and to abolish many of the old 'rotten boroughs'. More importantly, they wanted to extend voting rights to the middle-classes. Charles Fitzwilliam went so far as to advocate that no taxes should be paid until the Bill became law. This deliberate allusion to the 'No taxation without representation' policy of the American colonists of 60 years previously set the Tories back on their heels and the following derisive lines were penned:

> When wise Lord Milton fiercely screamed
> 'No taxes till the Bill is law'
> To all the Whigs Lord Milton seemed
> The noblest Lord they ever saw.[6]

On the death of his father in 1833, he surrendered his seat and became the 5th Earl Fitzwilliam. Two years later, his son William Thomas Spencer Fitzwilliam (the new Lord Milton) entered the Commons, holding a seat from 1837–41 and again from 1846–47 for Malton in Yorkshire. In 1847 he changed constituency and was MP for Wicklow from 1847 until his father's death in 1856, when he became the 6th Earl Fitzwilliam.

Chapter 2

LIFE ON THE COOLATTIN ESTATE 1830–1845

Despite the immense size of the Coolattin estate – approximately 80,000 acres – it was merely the Irish holding of the Fitzwilliam family. Their properties in England were of greater importance and the earls seldom visited County Wicklow.

Its day-to-day management was left in the hands of an agent. The Challoner family – Robert snr, succeeded by Robert jnr – held the position for many years in the first half of the nineteenth century. Strictly speaking, therefore, the Fitzwilliams were absentee landlords but the connotations which that description implies would be incorrect. Unlike the common absentee landlord, the Fitzwilliams were interested in the welfare of the estate. They were liberal in their dealings with their tenantry and their record of benign paternalism was evident in the way the estate was managed. Nevertheless, the Coolattin estate was a business and, like all businesses, it had to be viable. If the welfare of the estate and that of the tenants conflicted, the Fitzwilliams' first loyalty was to their property.

In 1844, the British government established a commission to study the system of land occupation in Ireland. It had been obvious for several decades that the proliferation of small holdings was a recipe for economic, and therefore social, disaster. This was the Devon Commission and in October of 1844 it focused its attention on County Wicklow. Leading

12

members of the rural community were invited to give evidence and the result was a snapshot of how large estates and their constituent small holdings operated. The evidence dealt with sizes of holdings, system of tenure, rents, head-tenants, sub-tenants, middlemen and cottiers, wages, affluence, poverty and other aspects of life in rural Wicklow at that time.

The Coolattin estate comprised 80,000 acres and was three times the size of the second largest estate in the region. It later grew to just under 90,000 acres. This vast area covered all the southwest of the county and isolated pockets of land elsewhere, amounting to almost one-fifth of the total area of Wicklow. The land was divided into farms and parklands, mountains and bogs. The 'big house' was at Coolattin Park near Shillelagh.

HOLDINGS

Beyond the environs of the demesne – the property immedi-ately surrounding the house which was not leased out – the land was parcelled out in farms varying in size from 700 or 800 acres down to a couple of acres. Many of the tenant farmers with large holdings sublet smaller lots and, in turn, many of the sub-tenants sublet portions of their holdings to those on a lower rung of the social ladder. At the bottom were landless labourers who merely rented a cabin and small garden.

In 1832 Challoner asked Fitzwilliam to introduce a ban on further subdivision of holdings 'except in the most urgent necessity as the larger class of farms is at present too small'. Fitzwilliam refused to sanction such a move and stated that each case would have to be reviewed independently.[1] Twelve years later, when giving evidence to the Devon Commission, Challoner still maintained that many of the holdings were 'smaller than they ought to be'. Another Devon Commission witness, Edward Burke, stated that there was a 'vast deal of

13

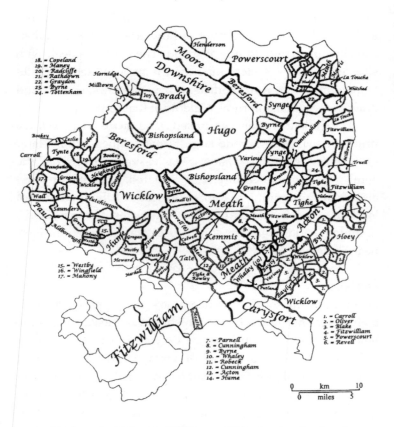

18. = Copeland
19. = Maney
20. = Radcliffe
21. = Rathdown
22. = Graydon
23. = Byrne
24. = Tottenham

15. = Westby
16. = Wingfield
17. = Mahony

7. = Parnell
8. = Cunningham
9. = Byrne
10. = Whaley
11. = Robeck
12. = Cunningham
13. = Acton
14. = Hume

1. = Carroll
2. = Oliver
3. = Blake
4. = Fitzwilliam
5. = Powerscourt
6. = Revell

*Landowners in County Wicklow, c. 1838, showing the size of
the Fitzwilliam holding in relation to other holdings
and the size of the county.*

small farms on the Fitzwilliam estate'. Subdivision had been a
problem but according to each of the witnesses it had been
greatly reduced. Challoner told the commission that 'subletting
does not continue if we can possibly help it'. When asked how
he prevented the continuance of the practice he answered: 'By
a good deal of talking.' Unfortunately, he wasn't asked to
elaborate.

TENURE

As mentioned above, many head-tenants, those who rented directly from Fitzwilliam, had sub-tenants. These secondary arrangements were not recognised by the estate, although the estate did sometimes take a conciliatory role in disputes. One such case was a disagreement between Mrs Chamney, a head-tenant at Ballyraghine (i.e., Ballyrahan) and one of her sub-tenants, Edward Byrne. Byrne had converted two out-offices on his holding into dwellings for the use of two sons who had recently married. Mrs Chamney gave the newly weds two months to quit the holding and the out-offices to be converted back to their original use. Byrne refused to comply with the directive and the matter was referred to Robert Challoner who, in turn, consulted with Fitzwilliam. Fitzwilliam agreed with Mrs Chamney.[2]

The head-tenants held their farms either under lease or at will. Leases were usually for 21 years and a life – whichever was the longer. The 'life' in a lease was a gamble. A named life might be that of a child. The longer the child lived, the longer the lease was valid. This policy had been introduced by Fitzwilliam around 1830. In the eighteenth century, it had been usual not to have any stated period but to take out a lease on three named lives, the lease expiring on the death of the last surviving nominee. Many of the tenants, and particularly the sub-tenants, had no lease. They were 'tenants-at-will' and had no security of tenure.

According to Fr Kavanagh, parish curate at Carnew, very few Catholics held property direct from Fitzwilliam but indirectly through the hands of Protestant middlemen. This could suggest an anti-Catholic bias on Fitzwilliam's part but two factors should be borne in mind. The first is the restrictions pertaining to land tenure imposed against Catholics by the eighteenth-century Penal Laws. These draconian laws had been introduced after the so-called 'Glorious Revolution' in which the Dutch Prince of Orange became King William of England in the 1690s, and they

15

completed earlier confiscation-and-redistribution policies which had the affect of transferring 95% of land in Ireland into Protestant hands. Secondly, the Fitzwilliams would have inherited the head-tenantry from the Rockinghams and were not responsible for its bias. Neither should it be forgotten that the Fitzwilliams had repeatedly displayed support for the rights of Catholics. It should also be pointed out that there were quite a few Protestant families who were close to the bottom stratum of society on the estate. Some were as poor as their Catholic neighbours. While this may suggest mobility (albeit downward mobility) within the social structure of the estate, few Catholic families managed upward mobility within a system designed to make such advancement extremely difficult.

Close scrutiny was kept on transactions involving leases. If a tenant wished to sell a lease, usually for about the equivalent of six years' rent, the sale could be completed only if Fitzwilliam approved of the purchaser. Likewise, if the widow of a lessee wished to re-marry, she could remain on the holding only if Fitzwilliam approved of her new husband. If he did not approve and she went ahead with the marriage she and her children might be turned out. According to Challoner, this was in the children's interest as there had been cases where the children of the second marriage were deemed to have a greater claim on the holding, leaving the children of the first marriage without a home. This was a contentious issue and Fr Kavanagh strongly objected to Fitzwilliam's interference in something as personal as the choice of a marriage partner.

Generally, those at the mercy of middlemen fared very badly compared to those who rented or leased directly from Fitzwilliam. Challoner told the commission that sometimes, when a tenant's lease expired, he intervened to put the sub-tenants' holdings on a 'proper footing', but he did not explain what he meant by this. In 1833, Fitzwilliam told Challoner that Dr Rhames, a head-tenant in the townland of

Gowle on the western edge of the estate, was not to exact too high a rent from his tenants. It is unclear how Challoner was to regulate this as the agreements between Rhames and his tenants were private. The only power the estate had in the matter was the threat of retribution when Rhames next had to negotiate his own lease from the estate.[3]

Many of the small-holdings were in joint names and this led to squabbles and disagreements. Few, if any, improvements took place on such holdings and most of the witnesses agreed that joint-holdings were not a good idea and should be eradicated.

RENT

The valuation of the various properties on the estate was fixed in 1834 by a Mr Bingley, an Englishman who had been brought over by Fitzwilliam for the purpose. Both Bingley and Challoner, and an unidentified Mr Matthew, wanted a drastic overhaul of leasing agreements giving the estate more control during the period of a lease than had been the case but Fitzwilliam was anxious that the tenants should not be made afraid of the estate.[4] It would appear that he held the view that further erosion of their independence would not be beneficial either to the tenants nor to the estate.

Bingley's valuation was generally fixed at 25 shillings an acre. Fitzwilliam felt that was too high and reduced the rent in most cases. Several witnesses at the Devon Commission testified that rents on the Fitzwilliam estate were generally lower than those elsewhere. However, the middlemen, the tenants who sublet to smallholders and labourers, charged far more than they were charged by the estate, thereby making substantial profits. The landless labourer paid £1 a year for his house. For another £1 he could have a kitchen garden and for £10 a year extra he would be given an acre or so of land on which he could grow potatoes. The estate had nothing to do with these unfortunate people who rented from the middle stratum. In reality, seldom, if ever, did money change hands between the cottier and the sub-tenant, the rent for the house and potato patch being paid in labour.

The rent was paid twice yearly. The year started on 25 March, Lady Day, and the first six months expired on Michaelmas, 29 September. But there was a breathing space before payment had to be made. Rent due in September did not have to be paid until December and that due in March could run until May. Despite this, many of the smallholders found it difficult to meet their responsibilities and had to borrow heavily from the loan funds.

The loan funds were universally despised. Abraham Tate, a landed proprietor and County Coroner, said: 'They (the loan funds) are barbarous. There are seven loan funds within thirteen miles of my house. They are the destruction of this country ... it is disgraceful to see the unfortunate creatures of the country going about to the different loan banks and getting money from one to pay another and going to the bank at Carnew and getting bills discounted at an enormous rate of interest. I always set my face against loan funds. I never conversed with a poor man yet who had got into a loan fund and did not say that it was his ruin; having got into it he could never get out of it.'

Robert Challoner had more-or-less the same to say, adding that he would like to close the one in Carnew, even though it had been started by his father, an advocate of the system. All the witnesses condemned the loan funds because of their exorbitant rate of interest, believing that local money-lenders were more reasonable to deal with.

Rent arrears were very common, some were allowed to accumulate over several years, amounting to hundreds of pounds, but the defaulters were seldom evicted by Fitzwilliam. On 25 March, 1830 an account of arrears – 'being such as are doubtful of ever being received' – amounted to £8,965-2-5.[5]

IMPROVEMENTS

Improvements to farm buildings and the land generally were always a tricky subject. This was particularly true when the improvements were of a permanent nature. After all, why should a tenant, even one with a 21-year lease, go to the expense of draining his holding or erecting a barn or extending his house if there was no guarantee that his lease would be renewed on expiration? Tenants-at-will were even more insecure and less likely to invest in the future of their holdings. This situation prevailed throughout Ireland.

Fitzwilliam was, once again, more enlightened than many of his peers. Sometimes Fitzwilliam footed the bill completely. When he did, he levied a 4–5% surcharge on the tenant's rent. On other occasions, carrying out improvements was a joint venture between the estate and the tenant, in which case the percentage surcharge was very low or not imposed at all. Usually such joint ventures entailed Fitzwilliam supplying the materials and the tenant supplying the labour. If the nature of the improvement was land drainage a 5% surcharge was added.[6] The general guideline set down by Fitzwilliam for Challoner was: 'In the case where a lessee has still a very great interest in a holding it is impossible for a landlord to lay out money in building or other permanent improvements unless the lessee consent(s) to add to the existing rent an adequate percentage of the outlay.'[7]

EMPLOYMENT

The landless labourers, of which there were many on the estate, were at the bottom of the social and economic ladder. According to Abraham Tate, since the gradual transfer to tillage farming in the region, farmers were employing three times as many agricultural labourers as they used to. Nevertheless, there were far more labourers than work available with the result that wages were kept to a minimum and many of the labourers lived in appalling conditions. Fr Kavanagh believed that 'the labouring class are not generally occupied or engaged ... there are numbers who cannot get employment, of the most honest and industrious character, so that we were called upon in the village of Carnew, in order to prevent starvation, to raise a fund to employ them'. And that was the year before the outbreak of the potato blight that was to lead to the Great Famine.

Wages averaged 10d (4p) per day in summer. This was reduced to 6d if the employer provided food. In winter 2d per day was knocked off because of the shorter daylight hours. The highest wages were paid by Fitzwilliam who, according to Challoner, gave one shilling a day, which Challoner felt was too much. By 1848, Challoner's own salary was £1,000 per annum, approximately 70 times that of a labourer's wage which he considered excessive.[8] Edward Burke stated that some employers paid as little as 6d a day without food and 4d if food was provided.

In 1836, eight years before the above figures were given to the Devon Commission, the labourers directly employed at Coolattin Park applied for an increase in wages. In their application they stated that they were strangers to every food except potatoes and had only 10d per day while those around them had higher wages and less labouring employment. Challoner protested that a great many of the applicants were being paid one shilling a day and that no labourers working 'on other farms around here' have more than 10d per day. Fitzwilliam's reply was that those labourers working on the Coolattin Park farm receiving 10d per day were to be given a 6d loaf every Saturday evening for the next six months but that no person who had not worked a full week would be entitled to the loaf.

Fitzwilliam made it clear, however, that this stipulation was 'not to be construed rigidly in the case of Catholics absent on (religious) holidays'.[9]

As stated above, labourers working for sub-tenants often gave their labour in lieu of paying rent for their cabins and kitchen gardens.

GENERAL CONDITIONS

A Farming Society had been established on the estate in 1830 but fourteen years later its efficacy was doubtful. It was generally agreed that it had brought improvements in farming practices. In particular, ploughing skills and animal husbandry had shown great benefits. The extent of the improvements, however, was very subjective. Abraham Tate felt that there had been great improvements; Challoner felt there was some improvement but that many of the smallholders were in distress; Robert Smith conceded there were improvements but they were slow in coming and Edward Burke, who had been a member of the Society since its inception, found that improvements were few and far between and later stated that there had been no improvements at all.

Whatever the level of success of the Society, its existence once more testifies to Fitzwilliam's forward-looking approach to the management of the Coolattin estate. Admittedly, Challoner was the man in charge and he must be given credit for originating many and implementing all development projects on the estate. In 1832, he suggested that the estate should pay for the training of two or three young local men by agriculturalists in England in the improved methods of agriculture. Fitzwilliam immediately agreed.[10] In 1841, Fitzwilliam also agreed to a scholarship for the best student on the estate going to Dublin University.

Despite these measures, the evidence given to the Devon

Commission in 1844 showed that the lot of the poor on the estate deteriorated throughout the 1830s and continued to decline in the 1840s. Some witnesses painted a bleaker picture than others but it should be noted that, in general, the more optimistic remarks were expressed by people who had little contact with the poorer classes on a daily basis while members of the Roman Catholic clergy and others who were in constant touch with the bottom stratum of society stated that on many occasions the plight of the poor was becoming increasingly alarming.[11] In common with their counterparts throughout Ireland, the poorer tenants on the Fitzwilliam estate lived on a diet of potatoes, sometimes supplemented with buttermilk and occasionally with salt herrings.[12]

Robert Challoner did point out, however, that the lot of the labourers had greatly improved through the Temperance Movement.

RELATIONSHIP BETWEEN THE ESTATE AND TENANTS

Fitzwilliam was generally regarded as being a 'good' landlord. He was credited with paying higher wages and charging lower rents than many of his fellow landowners. He also not only allowed Catholic as well as Protestant churches on his estate but he even contributed towards their construction costs. Likewise, he encouraged his tenants to send their children to the schools on the estate. Some of these schools were wholly maintained by him, others were subsidised by the estate coffers.[13] He contributed towards houses for curates and donated sums varying from £10 to £25 for the poor of Newcastle, Rathdrum and Wicklow. When the 5th Earl succeeded the 4th in 1833, he consented to continue the annual subscriptions to charities his father had supported, such as the Institute for the Deaf and Dumb. He also agreed to subscribe £10 per annum to the Dispensary at Aughrim. Even though it was not on the estate, many of his tenants lived within its area of operation and he felt they would benefit from it.[14]

The estate also ran a Poor Shop. This was a savings club for the tenants and those who wished to be members could save as much or as little as their income allowed. Considering the number of tenant families on the estate, the membership of the Poor Shop was quite small, about 100 names in all, only fifteen of which were men. Individual savings over a year varied from two shillings to ten shillings. When the savers had accumulated the amounts they needed, they withdrew their savings to purchase what they had saved for. In the majority of cases, clothes and blankets were bought. Sometimes the cash was simply withdrawn to be spent how and where the saver wished. In 1834, for example, Anna Balance of Ballynultagh used her five shillings to pay a debt and part-pay for a blanket. It is interesting to note that the reason for the withdrawal was usually recorded.[15]

The Carnew curate, Fr Kavanagh, was not afraid to speak out when he felt the situation warranted it, yet even he took the opportunity to express to the Devon Commission on behalf of the Roman Catholics of the region 'our gratitude to Lord Fitzwilliam as being one of the most generous and munificent landlords'. In 1841, the newly-appointed parish priest of Killaveny, Fr Thomas Hore, requested not only a new site for a church to replace the dilapidated structure which then served as the parish church but also an increase in Fitzwilliam's donation of £100.[16]

Fitzwilliam undoubtedly felt a responsibility towards his tenants, but he felt a greater responsibility towards the survival of the estate for future generations of Fitzwilliams. He was merely a custodian and when there was a clash of interests between the welfare of the tenantry and the welfare of the estate, the tenants ended up losers.

EVICTIONS

As early as 1830, the 4th Earl embarked on a policy of consolidating some of the smaller units into larger ones. This meant that some of the tenants were evicted and their holdings taken over by another, usually a neighbouring, tenant. Landholders in the townland of Hillbrook, near Carnew, were issued with eviction notices. They called a meeting at which it was decided to bring the situation to the notice of Daniel O'Connell, the champion of the Irish tenant, in the House of Commons. Local tradition states that O'Connell replied stating that he would address a meeting outside Coolafancy church after Sunday mass and he requested that they bring their eviction notices with them. A short time later, armed with the notices he received from the tenants, O'Connell challenged Fitzwilliam's eldest son, Lord Milton, in the House of Commons. It is said that Fitzwilliam denied that any evictions were taking place on his estate. O'Connell repeated the challenge. Again, Fitzwilliam denied it, but when O'Connell produced the notices, Fitzwilliam reputedly said: 'As long as I live there will never be another tenant evicted from my estate.'[17]

The tradition goes on to state that the eviction notices were rescinded but other sources maintain that an estimated 1,530 people were served with eviction notices in the county at that time and about 800 of these were ejected from the Coolattin estate. These people were left to fend for themselves and they drifted into the towns, where they became destitute.[18] The following year, the same earl donated a total of £65 – a handsome sum at the time but a trifling amount to Fitzwilliam – to various charities in the county. It would be too simplistic to dismiss this as conscience money and probably more accurate to describe it as indicative of Fitzwilliam's ability to keep his charitable tendencies and his long-term management of the estate separate.

In 1831, Challoner wrote a memorandum to Fitzwilliam

suggesting that 'in consequence of amalgamating small-holdings, in the course of time it will be necessary to turn several families adrift'. The earl's son, Lord Milton who had been challenged by O'Connell the previous year in the Commons, warned that great caution must be used in carrying into effect a scheme of this kind.[19]

The estate records show that on 5 April 1831, a Mr Dempsey was paid £254 on account in payment of getting 'sundry persons' from the estate to America. On 26 April, Dempsey received a further £186 and the balance of £116 was paid on 16 May. This brought the total to £556. Using the price-per-emigrant charged during the major clearances seventeen years later, the number of emigrants involved in the Dempsey transactions was about 160.[20]

In 1842, the same Milton, then the 5th Earl Fitzwilliam, instructed that single people were not to receive assistance to emigrate.[21] This, of course, implies that assisted emigration from the estate was already in place. Two years later, at the Devon Commission inquiry, Challoner admitted that 'we take every opportunity we can to do so (i.e., clear the estate of unviable tenants). I look upon it as one remedy to ease the unemployment situation'. However, he added that 'consolidation of farms, with few exceptions, does not take place' and even in those exceptions it was only with the consent of the tenants that were being evicted. Edward Burke conceded that it was generally felt that Fitzwilliam evicted only as a last resort. This is borne out by the record books, which show many cases of tenants greatly in arrears being allowed to remain on their holdings after years of default.

Chapter 3

THE POOR LAW

In 1838, the London parliament passed the Poor Law (Ireland) Act. It was designed to alleviate the suffering of the poor, ignoring the actual problem of poverty. The parliamentarians felt that poverty was a state over which they had no control, a state with which they should not interfere. The Act was merely a measure to stem the flow of Irish poor into the cities of Britain.

Migrant workers from Ireland had always been welcomed when the seasons demanded a large, cheap labour force but the welcome was short-lived and the migrants were expected to return to Ireland when their work was complete. In the 1820s and 1830s, however, more and more migrants stayed in England. Many went directly to the industrial areas in search of employment, others made their way to cities after their seasonal work in rural districts had come to an end. Cities such as Liverpool and Manchester soon found that they contained large communities of Irish paupers. This did not please the local authorities, the ratepayers, or the indigenous workforces. The authorities had the administrative problems of looking after these immigrants and the cost of the scant welfare they received had to be met by local ratepayers. The influx of cheap labour also caused problems for the local workforce as it tended to lower wages in what was becoming increasingly an employer's market.

Britain was undergoing one of its worst periods of recession. Since the end of the Napoleonic Wars, the British economy had deteriorated at an alarming rate. As usual, the most vulnerable section of society, the poor, bore the brunt. From the Peterloo Massacre of 1819, throughout the 1820s and into the beginning of the 1830s, social unrest fomented and revolution seemed possible, if not imminent. If rebellion of the 'lower classes' was to be avoided, a complete overhaul of the Poor Law would have to be carried out.

There had been a system for relieving destitution in England since Elizabethan times but it was totally inadequate to meet the demands placed on it over 200 years after its structuring. However, the prevailing dogma of political economy dictated non-interference. Government measures to relieve the destitution of the poor would, it was believed, only encourage poverty and improvidence. Paupers would not work if they knew that the government would provide for their needs. Worse still, this laissez-faire approach to the national economy warned that government intervention would affect food prices and thereby distort the market – and the market was sacrosanct. It was governed by the laws of supply and demand which were regarded as an extension of the laws of nature and, therefore, the laws of God.[1] On the other hand, if the needs of the poor were not met through employment or relief, there was the ever-increasing threat that those needs would be satisfied by force.

Political theory gave way to practical expediency and Rev Thomas Whateley and George Nicholls were commissioned to draft the new Poor Law. Whateley and Nicholls had come to the attention of the authorities through their ability to dispense Poor Law relief with admirable economy. Their greatest qualification for the job was their reluctance to spend public money. They were instructed to make Poor Relief more widely available but to make it so repugnant that even the most needy would be reluctant to seek it.

The commission on the new Poor Law first sat in 1832 and two years later its proposals were passed into law. It was not extended to Ireland. The government was well aware that a national system of relief would have to be introduced here as well but they had no idea how to proceed, with the result that relief of the Irish poor was left in the hands of private charity, just as it had always been.

Eventually, the Protestant Archbishop of Dublin, Richard Whateley, was appointed to chair an enquiry into the plight of the poor in Ireland.[2] His findings surpassed everyone's greatest fears. He estimated that 30% of the entire population would need assistance for 30 weeks of each year. He advocated reclamation schemes of marginal land and development of the fisheries, but his most fervent proposal was government assisted emigration to the colonies. This echoed the beliefs of many of the leading economists that the overcrowded state of Ireland and its economic depression could only be rectified through emigration. There would also be the added benefit of populating the colonies of British North America (the Maritime Provinces and the Upper and Lower Canadas).[3] The very mention of assisted emigration smacked of hypocrisy in a system which advocated non-interference.

The government refused to accept that the situation in Ireland was as bad as Whateley reported and his findings were soon forgotten. Someone with a greater appreciation of the 'realities' of Poor Law requirements was needed. Not surprisingly, they turned to George Nicholls who had successfully drawn up the draconian Poor Law in England.

Nicholls completed his draft proposals in twelve weeks, only nine of which he spent in parts of Ireland reviewing the living conditions of the poor. His conclusions were that the

English system could be transplanted into Ireland with little or no regard to the vast economic structural differences which existed between the two countries. He also reported that Whateley's figure of 30% of the population in need of assistance was wildly exaggerated and that 1% was a truer figure. Before these proposals passed through parliament, however, Nicholls paid a second visit to Ireland. This time, he looked with less prejudicial eyes and conceded that the level of poverty was greater than he had previously thought. Nevertheless, apart from a few changes, his proposal to implement a Poor Law based on that of the English system passed through the various stages and became law in 1838.

Under this Poor Law (Ireland) Act, Ireland was divided into 130 administrative Poor Law Unions. The Unions were so-called because they were composed of a union of several electoral divisions within a district. Each of these Unions was run by a Board of Poor Law Guardians and the entire network was overseen from London by the Poor Law Commissioners. Nicholls and four other members of the English Poor Law Commission were appointed to run the Irish system.

The main work of the Guardians was to erect and maintain a workhouse (also known as a Poor House) in their respective Union. This was to be financed by a local levy on landowners – a 'rate'. Under this system, it was felt that the Irish ratepayers, and not English ratepayers, would be made responsible for the Irish poor. Throughout the country, these workhouses had a total accommodation for 100,000 paupers. They were bleak and forbidding. As the law had been designed to keep the Irish poor out of England, the harsh regime of the workhouse was designed to keep the number of people seeking admittance down to a minimum, thereby keeping the cost to the ratepayer down to a minimum. It should not be forgotten that all the Poor Law Guardians were recruited from the ranks of the ratepayers.

When destitute families were admitted to the workhouse they were split up, with men and boys in one wing, women and girls in the other. 'No contact was permitted between married couples. Parents were to have reasonable access to their children without inconveniencing the poorhouse administration'.[4] Inspectors appointed to monitor the running of these workhouses repeatedly reported cases of administrative inefficiency, neglect and corruption. Little was done to improve matters.

Under no circumstances was outdoor relief to be given. This, in effect, meant that nobody, no matter how destitute, had a right to assistance. To begin with, they had to be totally without means and must enter the workhouse to qualify for help. If the workhouse was full and no more admissions could be made then those left outside could still not be assisted.

THE SITUATION IN WICKLOW[5]

By comparison with counties west of the Shannon and other parts of Ireland, County Wicklow did not have a major poverty problem. Nevertheless, the plight of the Wicklow destitute was no less serious. The months between the last supplies of old crop potatoes and the harvesting of the new saw the destitute take to the roads in Wicklow just as anywhere else in Ireland. The need for a Poor Law system in the county was obvious.

Under the 1838 Act, the county was divided into five Poor Law Unions, all of which were established in the second half of 1839. In the northeast was Rathdown which was comprised mostly of electoral districts in south County Dublin. The workhouse there was situated at Loughlinstown. The north-west districts of Blessington and Baltiboys were incorporated into the Naas Union in County Kildare. Rathdrum Union looked after the southeast and Baltinglass Union looked after the west. The fifth Union was situated in the southwest of the county with Shillelagh as its centre-point. Within three years each union

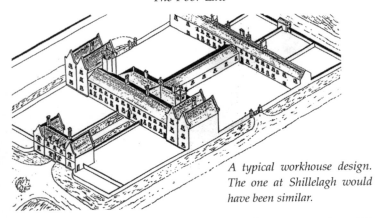

A typical workhouse design. The one at Shillelagh would have been similar.

had built its workhouse. Rathdown had room for 600 paupers, Rathdrum could also house 600, Baltinglass 500 and Shillelagh 400.

THE SHILLELAGH UNION

There was strong opposition to Nicholls' plan for an Irish Poor Law. The main platform was that Ireland's particular poverty problems could not be remedied by an off-the-peg solution. A tailor-made response was necessary. Others objected on the grounds that Ireland could not possibly afford the scheme. One of these was Lord Fitzwilliam.[6] Perhaps that was why, in 1841, some months before the Shillelagh Workhouse opened, Fitzwilliam refused to negotiate in giving, renting or leasing a residence in or near Shillelagh to the medical attendant of the Workhouse, Dr Bookey.[7] An interesting aspect about this Workhouse was its location. This Union was originally conceived as Tinahely Union and it would have followed the normal pattern had the Workhouse been placed in a centre of population such as Tinahely or Carnew but it was decided to place it right in the middle of the Coolattin estate in the tiny village of Shillelagh. Whatever about Fitzwilliam's initial misgivings, he obviously decided to make the best of the situation and by the late 1840s, he was chairman of the Shillelagh Union's Board of Guardians.

Chapter 4

CRISIS: 1845–6

THE PARTIAL FAILURE OF 1845

While it was generally agreed that Fitzwilliam was a 'good' landlord, the poorer tenants still lived in wretched conditions and endured a hand-to-mouth existence. It was life by brinkmanship and it would take very little to upset the delicate balance between subsistence and starvation. The autumn of 1845 brought the brink nearer.

In October, the first reports of potato blight in County Wicklow were made known. These were dismissed by the authorities as unfortunate but not unduly disturbing. Scarcely a year went by without blight appearing in some region of Ireland. More widespread crop failures had been experienced in most decades since the 1780s. The distress caused by the 1845 failure, it was felt, would not be very much worse than usual. More reports came in and by November it was clear that the scale of the problem was greater than originally suspected but still threatening nothing that had not been dealt with before.

As the new year dawned, local relief committees were established to help those on the bottom rung of the economic ladder to get over the food shortage. Some areas were hit worse than others but it was the urban dwellers who were among the first to feel the effects as the threatened shortage sent food prices spiralling. The tenants on the Fitzwilliam estate escaped the worst of the blight with an estimated two-thirds to four-fifths of the crop undamaged.

Throughout the spring of 1846, reduced availability of cheap food and the resultant high prices of what remained caused great distress but there was still no reason to believe that this was the preamble to the greatest social catastrophe in Irish history. As one historian has written: '... had the potato famine of 1845 lasted just one year it would probably have merited no more than a few paragraphs in the history books'.[1]

With the arrival of the new planting season, there was no reason to suspect a repeat failure. With this in mind, County Wicklow farmers and labourers planted 14,861 acres of potatoes, a decrease of less than 12% of the acreage planted the previous year. On the Fitzwilliam estate confidence in a good crop was reflected in the fact that about 95% of the usual acreage was planted. Such optimism was to prove misplaced and the summer and autumn heralded a disaster of unparalleled proportions.

THE ANNIHILATION OF THE 1846 CROP

As early as July and August the stench that was to become so familiar filled the air. At first, isolated reports of blight trickled in from various parts of the county but it soon became a torrent that showed that this time nowhere had been spared. Not only was it more widespread than the previous year but the extent of the corruption was greater. This was annihilation of the basic foodstuff of the vast majority of the rural poor. The little that survived would be so expensive that few would be able to afford it.

In the emergency caused by the partial failure of the previous year, the government had opened relief work schemes for the destitute but these had given rise to complaints that landlords and other private individuals had profited by this expenditure of public money. This criticism heightened the government's eagerness to halt the schemes as soon as the new crop was ready for harvesting. The scaling down was well advanced when the complete failure of the new crop was discovered. It was obvious that not only would the relief works have to be retained but they would have to be extended to cope with the catastrophe that lay ahead. The government, despite their obsessive but selective reluctance to interfere in the natural course of the labour market, admitted that there was no option but to re-open the schemes. However, conscious of the criticism that private benefit had accrued from such work schemes, they devised new rules. Only areas where distress was greatest would be allocated relief projects. This meant that the various relief committees would have to prepare submissions for consideration. This would take time – time which the destitute could ill-afford. While procedures were adhered to the food shortage crisis worsened.

At the beginning of September 1846, the various relief committees in and around the Fitzwilliam estate submitted their completed questionnaires which had been drafted by the Poor Law Commissioners. Henry Braddle (or Braddell as it was spelt in some of the Fitzwilliam Papers) of Ballingate completed the questionnaire for the Carnew area. He said that the labouring people there depended on the potato and a little oatmeal for their diet. He believed that there was not enough food to get them beyond November. There was no work available nor did any seem likely. There were no public work schemes established there. Rev Fetherstone of Moyne, Abraham Tate of Ballintaggart, Captain Nixon of Tullow, Ralph Hope of Urelands, Eaton Taylor of Ballyconnell, John Lawrie (Fitzwilliam's agriculturist at Coolattin) and Fr Hore of Killaveny all had more-or-less the same to say. There was no work, there was no likelihood of work and relief projects were urgently needed if the people were not to starve. In none of these regions would the potato stock last beyond December.[2] On 14 September, Thomas de Renzy, a Justice of the Peace living near Carnew, wrote to the Relief Commissioners attaching a memorial signed by 75 local men stating that the cost of available food had risen so quickly and steeply that even those who were working could no longer afford to buy it in sufficient quantities.[3]

The tenants of the Fitzwilliam estate, in common with their counterparts in other parts of the county and throughout Ireland, were faced with starvation. The harvest was a putrid mass of corruption, the stench of which permeated the countryside. The fertile grassy lowlands bore the same mark of disaster as the craggy districts of the hills and mountains. Nowhere escaped. The poor threw themselves on the mercy of the workhouse.

The workhouses had been designed to discourage admission but as the winter of 1846/7 deepened, the horrific conditions outside their walls left the people without hope or alternative. The workhouses throughout Wicklow were soon full to overflowing. The Shillelagh workhouse had been designed to accommodate 400 inmates. It was declared full on 12 December. In the towns, soup kitchens had been opened but these were inaccessible to people who lived any distance from them, especially people who were in an already weakened state. The only hope of salvation lay in the work schemes.

These continued to provide some relief for the thousands of destitute people in the south-west corner of the county but like the workhouses, they were overcrowded. On one two-and-a-half mile stretch of road near Tinahely there were 570 men receiving one shilling a day.[4] This was the same as the wage paid by Fitzwilliam, which was generally considered to be the highest in the region, but the spiralling cost of food had eroded its purchasing power so that it was grossly inadequate. This inadequacy was manifest by the fact that men who joined the

Despite their austerity, the workhouses were soon filled to overflowing,
leaving many of the destitute with nowhere to go.

schemes in reasonable health were soon gaunt figures unable
to carry out the work required of them. It was not unknown
for deaths to take place on the relief works. It looked as if the
situation could not get any worse but it did.

On 6 February, snow fell heavily throughout Wicklow,
blocking many roads, particularly those in remote areas. Lt
John Anderson was the Poor Law Inspecting Officer for the
county and he submitted a particularly disturbing report on 9
February. He had been travelling from Rathdrum to Moyne
when the way became impassible because of the snow drift.
He had 'literally to dig the horse out at places' and could get
no further than Sheanna. There was little food in that district
and he saw scant hope of getting supply carts through under
the conditions he had encountered. He had no doubt that
starvation faced the local population. 'One family (is) lying in
bed as they have no food or fuel. I fear these and many others
would perish were it not for private benevolence and in this
mountainous wild district it is to be feared that many, many
will perish unheard of.'[5]

When spring came it brought with it the thaw and a new
planting season, but the men on the schemes were reluctant to

leave them. Bad as they were, the schemes offered regular income. The buying power of the wages they received from the works may well have been eroded but the local farmers could not offer more. It is understandable that having endured a partial potato crop failure followed by an almost total failure, these people were intent on clinging to whatever security they had. The government decided that the only way to get the men off the relief works and back into the fields was to bring the schemes to an end. They decreed that a 20% reduction of numbers would have to be effected from 20 March and that all schemes were to close completely by 1 May. Once again, political expediency ignored logic. How were the people to survive the potato growing period between the time of sowing the crop and the time of harvesting it?

In Carnew a subscription list for the local soup kitchen showed that by 27 March £40-5-6 had been donated. It is interesting that £20 of this total had been received from Fitzwilliam and £5 from Robert Challoner. Challoner was a tireless worker for the local committees, being treasurer of three of them. Such measures, though welcome, were not the answer. A major overhaul of the Poor Law was required to fill the void. That overhaul came in 1847 as the Poor Law Amendment Act.

The two most important changes in the Act were the granting of outdoor relief and the infamous Gregory Clause. From the point of view of immediate widespread benefit, the provision of outdoor relief for the first time was of immense value. Under the existing regulations, only inmates of the workhouses could receive food or other assistance but the fact that hundreds of thousands of destitute people could not get into the workhouses because they were already full meant that the majority of paupers in dire need could not receive state aid. It was obvious that this anomaly had to be rectified but there was still a vociferous lobby who opposed it. More far-reaching in the mid- and long-term was the Gregory Clause. William Gregory was the Conservative MP for Dublin. He proposed that anyone in possession of a quarter-acre holding or more should be ineligible for any relief under the Poor Law provisions. Such holders, irrespective of how little food they had or were likely to have, would have to surrender their plots to their landlords before they would be helped. The Gregory Clause, coupled with another amendment by which landlords were further taxed on plots with a valuation of less than £4, was the catalyst by which estate clearances were immediately brought into play.

Such clearances had been contemplated for some time but this piece of legislation left landlords with little choice but to round up uneconomic tenants and eject them not only from their holdings but to facilitate their emigration out of Ireland. Even the most benign of landlords, whose income from rents had dwindled dramatically since the outbreak of the potato blight, could not ignore the crippling effects of these amendments. This was especially true of the bigger landlords, who now found it more expedient to export the problem across the Atlantic.

Chapter 5

SHEDDING THE SURPLUS

Sometime in early February 1847, word circulated around Coolattin that volunteers were needed for emigration. Either the scheme was announced and candidates invited to put their names forward or selected tenants were approached by the estate representatives. The fact that the entries in the Emigration Books follow no geographical pattern would suggest the former method, with tenants coming from all parts of the estate and having their names entered as they arrived at a designated registration centre. On the other hand, some of those listed refused to go, which indicates that not all candidacies were voluntary.[1] Speculation among the tenantry was rife. What terms would be offered? What choices would be given? One thing was certain, while they could be made leave the estate, they could not be forced out of the country. So the biggest question of all was, if offered passage to Canada, should they take it or simply stay in Ireland and hope things would improve?

Thomas Free of Kilcavan, near the village of Carnew, was tempted. Free was an industrious man with seventeen acres which he held by lease granted eight years earlier at £10-15-0 per annum. He had improved his house and land. Nevertheless, the estate felt that he and his family were suitable candidates for emigration. The family consisted of his wife Mary, eldest son Robert (his age was not recorded), Mary, junior, who was eighteen, Samuel who was sixteen, thirteen-year-old Thomas and eight-year-old Eliza. It was agreed that 24-year-old Mary Reilly, perhaps a relative, could travel with them. They were the first of over 300 families to be entered in the estate's Emigration Book over the next month or six weeks.[2]

The second entry in the Emigration Book shows how widespread the process was to be, both geographically and in regard to the social standing of the tenants. The Free family had seventeen acres which put them a couple of rungs up the scale. The Keeleys were quite different. Daniel Keeley and his extended family of ten held a cabin and small 'kitchen garden' from John Sheppard, a head-tenant of the estate, in the townland of Liscolman. The term kitchen garden was used throughout the Emigration Books and, in all probability, euphemistically referred to a potato patch with perhaps a few other assorted vegetables. His house was to come down. This was usually the case and was intended to prevent tenants who had left the estate from returning to their former homes or to prevent anyone else from moving in on their departure. People who knocked down these abandoned cabins were paid five shillings by the estate. Departing tenants were given the option of doing the work themselves.

It is not difficult to imagine the scene in any of the homes affected. There were reasons for joy, despair, courage and fear. There were reasons for hope and regret. The younger ones would embrace the opportunity while the older ones would be less sanguine. Why should they stay where the value of land was dissipating with each successive season, where work was becoming increasingly rare and wages increasingly useless? At worst, this seemed to offer an escape; at best, it was their chance of a new life where effort and toil would be rewarded. But what dangers lay in the wilds of Canada? Which was the greater, the disheartening experience of a sad past and a hopeless present or the fear of an unknown future? For many, the answer lay in their children. No matter what adversity awaited them in the unknown, it could not be worse than what Ireland had to offer. Now, Lord Fitzwilliam was making it possible for anyone who wished to go to do so. Some families on the estate, such as the Hopkins of Corndog and the Cuffes of Askakeagh, already had relatives who had made their way to Canada in the previous decade or two. They would know a little about what might be expected. Their advice would be sought and such emigrants' letters home would, no doubt, have assumed a wider and more immediate significance.

Without fuller information, it is difficult to determine all the criteria which qualified people for the scheme. There were many cases of individuals not being allowed to accompany their families to Canada. In some instances, this was understandable, if a little callous, in that a fourteen or fifteen-year-old son or daughter might be working away from home and was, therefore, not regarded as being dependent on the estate. But what of young children whose names were first added to the list and then scratched off? Why were they rejected? Perhaps in a few cases they had died between the time their names had been given and the time of departure. There were quite a few 'foundlings' and in most of these cases supporting evidence that the child had been cared for by the family had to be produced.

Any land holding, whether it consisted of a kitchen garden, one acre or 50, was to be incorporated into larger neighbouring holdings. In some cases, the recipient of the holding was expected to pay at least some of the costs of emigrating the departing family. For example, Mr Brewster of Ballynultagh agreed to pay half of the expenses of sending John Byrne and his family to Canada because he was to take over Byrne's six acres. In the majority of cases incorporation simply meant that the sublet holdings reverted to the immediate lessor.

41

In other parts of Ireland, tenants who increased their holdings by incorporating the holdings of evicted or otherwise departing tenants were sometimes ostracised by the local community but this does not seem to have happened on the Coolattin estate. Perhaps it was the fact that unadorned eviction was not usually resorted to by Fitzwilliam.

PASSAGE AND SUPPORT

Fitzwilliam would have been within his rights to evict any and all tenants who were in arrears with rent. He could also bring pressure to bear on those tenants who had sublet to evict their tenants. However, some encouragement to surrender their holdings would have to be given to those in good standing with regard to their rent. The clearances, therefore, were brought about by the dual expedients of stick-and-carrot.

The stick was the threat of immediate or eventual eviction with the prospect of the workhouse looming in the background. The carrot was the promise of a new life in Canada with passage paid and 'support'. Support meant different things to different families. For example, some families were allowed ten shillings per family member. Others received fifteen shillings a head for those who were prepared to travel. There were also cases of families being given an agreed sum (£20 in one instance) to buy clothes and provisions. Richard Hatch of Cronelea received £10 support on surrendering his 23 acres. Some families who had carried out improvements on their holdings negotiated terms on surrendering their property. The Hinch family of Killabeg did well in getting a £40 settlement for their five acres and 'a good house'. The family consisted of 30-year-old John and his four sisters and the £40 was made up as £16-15-0 passage (i.e., £3-7-0 each), £7-0-0 support, and a cash settlement of £16-5-0. Others, such as Michael Carty of Ardoyne, wanted payment for vacating the land and the growing crop instead of passage and support. William Byrne, who held 43 acres in Munny, wanted 'something in addition to passage and support' despite the fact that he was three years in arrears with rent.

There were also cases in which passage only was allowed and not everyone was even offered that. If the head of a family wanted to take someone who was not his or her biological child he or she would have to find the passage fare for that child. For example, in 1853 Fr Synnott, the parish priest of Killaveny/ Annacurra, had to make a written statement supporting Anne Lynch's claim that she had been nursing a deserted child for four years and that she was willing to pay the child's fare if the child was allowed to go to Canada with her.[3]

The ship was due to sail from New Ross at the beginning of April. Once the emigrants had made their decision to leave, much had to be done before setting out on a voyage from which there would be little likelihood of return. Relatives and friends would have to be notified, goodbyes said. Anything that could not be brought was to be sold. Each family was permitted a chest into which they crammed as much as they could. These chests were paid for by the estate.

Throughout March, over 300 families planned and looked to the future. Their leave-taking would split families forever and not everyone wanted to go. The old and infirm were particularly reluctant to face the rigours and dangers that lay ahead. Pragmatically, everyone knew who could not or should not go but family loyalty would scream that to leave them behind was a sin against nature. How could adult children desert aged parents, even when those very parents urged them to do so? How could brothers and sisters leave infirm siblings to cope in situations from which the able-bodied were hoping to escape? Such were the warring emotions which made emigration so traumatic, so soul-rending.

The First Stage: To New Ross

As March came to a close, over 2,000 men, women and children left their homes in County Wicklow and headed south towards the port of New Ross, some 60 miles away in south-west Wexford. It was the first step in a long journey. No ship leaving a small port like New Ross could accommodate so many, so they were divided into several shiploads, each with a specified date for embarkation.

On the day of departure from their homes, friends and relatives came to wish the emigrants well. Emotion was high. There was little room for joy. There is a print from 1851 which shows a family surrounded by well-wishers as they are about to leave their home forever.[4] It sums up the scene as no words could. The central figure is the local priest, giving his blessing to help strengthen their resolve in the trying times ahead. In the distance can be seen groups who have already begun the long walk to the port from which they would sail. Two small children cry as they bid farewell to their pet dog and in the middle of the scene, a horse-drawn cart is being loaded with the few belongings the emigrants can take with them. It was a scene that was to be acted out again and again across the Coolattin estate and across Ireland.

The journey to New Ross was on foot. The carts provided and driven by relatives, friends or neighbours, carried the luggage or the young or old when they became tired. In some cases the estate provided carriage costs. Starting early, they walked throughout the day, taking them further from the lives they had known and towards what they could merely guess at. For unspecified reasons, some families did not emigrate as scheduled and their names can be found listed in 1847 and again in 1848 or one of the other subsequent years. Daniel Keeley and his family were a case in point. Originally scheduled to leave in 1847, they appear again in the following year's list but the

Emigration scenes such as these were enacted throughout the estate.

surname is spelled Kealey. Perhaps an illness had delayed them or perhaps they simply succumbed to the temptation to hold on for just one more year. Whenever they left, the journey was the same. As darkness fell, they would stop by the road and rest as best they could, chatting, lying quietly. Then would come the dawn. They would eat and set out on the second day. If all went well, they just might make New Ross the following day.

Challoner had sent one of his leading hands with them, Ralph Lawrenson, to make sure that there were no problems and all would board the ship. The firm of Graves and Co. owned and operated ships which traded between US and Canadian ports and those in Britain and Ireland. They chartered other ships when needed and were experienced in the carriage of goods such as timber from Canada and tobacco, molasses and cotton from the United States. In common with other shipping agents, in recent years they had become equally experienced in sending those ships back across the Atlantic loaded with people. The usual routine was an eastward voyage from

Canada or the US to Liverpool where the cargo was discharged before the vessel sailed in ballast for New Ross where she would take on emigrants for the return journey. Graves would reap the benefit of the mass exodus which the estate now planned.

So much has been said and written about 'coffin ships' that it is easy to forget that such dilapidated vessels constituted only a tiny percentage of ships used in the emigrant trade. They did exist but not in the numbers which are generally believed. Most of the ships used to take famine emigrants across the Atlantic were rough and ready, general cargo ships with the barest of modification for the accommodation of passengers. Comfort was not a consideration, but the ships themselves were seaworthy. Tales of rotten hulks crammed with destitute refugees being sent to sea for insurance gain may reflect isolated cases but the vast majority of emigrant ships were strong and well capable of making two round trips during the spring-to-autumn season. The efficient running of the ships depended a great deal on the honesty of the agent, the level of concern of an influential sponsor and ultimately the character of the masters and crews. In the case of the Fitzwilliam tenants, both the honesty of Graves and the concern of Fitzwilliam guaranteed ships which were among the best available.

When their names had been checked against the passenger list which Graves had received from Challoner, the emigrants settled down to wait. If the ship was in port ready to board they would do so and if not they would wait until she arrived and embarkation could begin.

Chapter 6

LIFE IN THE 'TWEEN DECKS

The ship to take the first batch of Fitzwilliam tenants in this clearance programme was the *Dunbrody*. For many, it was their first time to see a large ship, the masts reaching ever upward, the spars crossed, the sails furled. Once on deck, they would be directed to the hatchway which led to the 'tween decks which was to be their home for the next four, five, six or more weeks. Though five weeks was the average duration, who could tell how long the voyage would take, as sailing ships were at the whim of the weather?

Once they headed down the gangway into the dark world of the ship's cargo hold, rough boards formed two tiers of bunks six feet square. To the uninformed, such allocation of space did not seem too bad, but the bunks were not intended for the exclusive use of a single passenger, nor were they to be shared by two people, nor even three. Four passengers were to crowd into this six-foot-by-six space. Each was allocated six-feet-by-eighteen inches, a mere nine square feet to call their own until they reached Quebec. Large families claimed adjacent bunks, smaller ones and people travelling alone no doubt sought out the close proximity of friends. Such sleeping arrangements could prove disturbing for young women and men travelling alone and various government committees investigating conditions on board emigrant ships repeatedly

Roll call. Once this was complete, no one could go ashore.

heard of activities between unmarried people of both sexes leading to 'bad results'. Even when getting undressed for bed it was extremely difficult to maintain privacy and the voyeuristically inclined were often well rewarded for vigilance. Not surprisingly, many women spent the first nights of the voyage sitting up, fully dressed. Eventually fatigue triumphed over decorum. Perhaps one of the advantages the Fitzwilliam tenants had was the fact that families, friends and former neighbours were all travelling together and the more vulnerable passengers were looked after rather than peered at.

Chests were stowed where they could be seen, or used as proprietory markers and, in that dismal catacomb, the people made their spaces as much their own as they could. The narrow passageways between the tiers of bunks were common space to be left clear but in such confinements even this would have been cluttered.

The trickle of emigrants from Britain to the United States and Canada in the first three decades of the century had not been significant enough to warrant the attention of, or regulation by, government. As the numbers began to greatly increase, however, the wretched conditions they suffered en route were drawn more and more into the public arena. Philanthropists, social reformers, churchmen and emigrants themselves wrote to newspapers, published pamphlets and did whatever they felt they had to do to get the government to regulate the emigrant trade. Not surprisingly, there was an equally vociferous lobby against such interference. This was the 'free-market-is-the-will-of God' brigade which comprised of shipowners, their agents, boarding house owners, tavern keepers and everyone else who was making money out of the sordid business. There was also a small group who honestly felt that the rigours of an ocean voyage were being exaggerated. After all, some claimed they had crossed the Atlantic several times and had been invigorated by the experience. On the whole, they seem to have been well-meaning if ridiculously naïve. Those who had, as they claimed, sailed the Atlantic had done so as cabin passengers whose elegant quarters were on deck. Few, if any, of them had travelled steerage and therefore had little idea of the horrors endured by passengers below deck.

THE PASSENGER ACTS

The increased publicity intensified cries for reform. The ludicrously lax and unenforced Passenger Acts of 1803 and 1823 were dusted off and scrutinised and new regulations were introduced in 1842. These were not much better. The number of people allowed per ship was three per five registered tons. So if a 500 ton ship was used, she was licensed to carry 300 people. This total included the crew. If the crew complement was 25, 275 passengers could be squeezed on without breeching the laws designed for their health and safety. To compound this sardine-syndrome, children under the age of fourteen were considered to be

'Steerage' –the 'tween decks accommodation.

half-adults, while infants under one year were not counted at all. The inclusion of infants and older children could easily bring the actual head count to well in excess of the official figure.

As for provisions, each passenger was entitled to three-quarts of water per day and seven pounds of bread, biscuit, flour, oatmeal or rice per week. Potatoes could be substituted for some of the bread. This weekly allowance was to be served at convenient times, not less than twice a week. They were to be provided not only for the duration of the voyage but for up to 48 hours after the ship's arrival at the port of destination, if there was a delay disembarking for quarantine or any other reason. The quantities were generally agreed to be sufficient to prevent starvation but little else and passengers were advised to carry their own stock of food on the voyage. The Fitzwilliam estate provided departing tenants with oatmeal and rice.

The bunks and personal space described were the dimensions stipulated in the act as minimum. The height between decks was to be at least six feet. The provision of lifeboats on board ships was to be as follows: ships of 150–250 tons burden (or 90–150 passengers and crew) two boats; 251–500 tons (or 150–300 passengers and crew) three boats; 500+ tons, four boats. Another provision of the Act was that no alcohol was to be sold to passengers. A breach of this would result in a fine of £100 against the ship's master.

These measures, inadequate as they were, were regularly breached. The necessary funding to enforce them did not materialise and, consequently, the necessary increase in the number of emigration officers or other government officials at the ports did not take place. Those who were conscientious enough in their duty to try to enforce the new regulations simply could not cope with the demand and this was before the flood gates of emigration burst open after 1846. To give one example of how these laws were flouted, many captains looked on the sale of liquor on board as one of their perks of command.

Finally, two copies of the Act were to be kept on board to be produced for inspection by any passenger who requested them.[1]

DOWN THE BARROW

While the crew prepared the ship for sea, and all stores and cargo safely stowed, the emigrants settled into their allotted spaces, the passengers could, within reason, still go ashore. It would be weeks before they could again enjoy a stroll and breathe fresh air that was not heavily laden with salt. Once the final head-count had been conducted, however, and the ship was in the final stages of preparation, they must stay on board. By this time, the last farewell from friends and loved ones, who had accompanied them to New Ross and who would stay until the ship could no longer be seen, had taken place. With the casting off of lines for'ard and aft, all that remained was the hopeless reaching of hands down from the ship's rail towards hands stretching upwards from the dockside, rigid fingers screaming for one last touch. Only the young, or those who had no one to wish them goodbye, bore the signs of embarking upon a great adventure.

The last farewell.

Slowly, the vessel was pulled out into the river by the small steam tug that would take her a few miles downstream. The shouts and sobs exchanged between those who were leaving and those who were staying continued. As long as they did not get in the way of the crew, who would have had little to do while the ship was still under tow, the passengers would be allowed to remain on deck, drinking in their final views of an Irish landscape. On the portside, to the east, lay County Wexford and to starboard lay County Kilkenny. Fertile fields undulated gently in either direction.

For about four miles the gradual widening of the river was almost imperceptible, then, as if the gentle waters had burst their banks, it opened out to twice its breadth. It was at this point that the crew, as if appearing from nowhere, jumped to the barked orders of the boatswain, who echoed the calls of the mate. In well-practised order, detachments took up positions at various posts along the deck. When all was prepared, the order to unfurl the sails was barked out, the gaskets which kept them furled were opened and the white canvas sheets fell open and billowed in the breeze. The tug would stand by for a few moments until satisfied its task was over, when it would then steam back upriver.

The river bank fell further away now and the expanse of water became more saline than fresh. This was the wide, deep inlet known as Waterford harbour. As they neared Cheekpoint, the ruins of an ancient church on the Wexford side watched the ship's stately progress. This was the once proud Dunbrody Abbey, after which the ship was named.

There was a difference in the air now. It was salty and the breeze was fresher, unhindered by hedgerows and hills. Within another hour, at most, the ship would reach the end of the inlet and the open sea would be encountered.

CROSSING THE ATLANTIC

Once at sea, the slow tenor of life would establish itself. If the weather was fine, the rolling motion would be unpleasant for only the most sensitive stomach. The passengers would be allowed on deck at specific times on condition they did not hamper the work of the crew. There were also the cabin passengers to consider as they would have paid a great deal more than the steerage emigrants and they should be able to promenade on deck without having to mingle with the 'great unwashed'. While access to the deck was restricted for steerage passengers, the hatches would be left open and air could circulate to some extent at least. In such conditions, particularly in the early stages of a voyage, there was a certain amount of optimism as the ship sailed westward, leaving Ireland in her wake. This progress towards a new beginning put the passengers in a healthier frame of mind and they made their own entertainment. Among so many, the presence of musicians was not uncommon and possessions were pushed out of the way to allow whatever dancing

Dancing between decks.

space could be made. Such diversion was not only welcomed but encouraged by shipowners and masters. It kept the emigrants amused and took their minds off the cramped conditions. For the dancers, at least, it also provided a form of exercise.

However, if the weather was foul, the passengers were put below and the hatches covered. Once out on the ocean, the ship would toss and pitch and it would not be long before the coughing and retching would be heard throughout the steerage accommodation. Few, if any, would be spared the agonies of seasickness. The air would become thick with the stench of vomit. The absence of sufficient buckets or other containers into which they could puke left them no option but to let it spill where it would. Emptied stomachs would rebel again and again until nothing, not even bile, remained. Strength gone, they moaned pitifully, as they lay huddled in corners or prostrate in their bunks, which they shared with three fellow passengers, all tightly packed together and all suffering each other's sickness. Those in the lower tiers were doubly unfortunate, for not only did they lie in their own sick and dirt but they also had to endure the vomit and excrement of those above as it dribbled through the planks of the upper bunks. Even if the voyage started well, there was the almost certain knowledge that such a scene awaited all who would venture across the Atlantic ocean in steerage.

There was no shortage of advice on the prevention and cure for seasickness. Most of them were hare-brained, concocted by cranks and charlatans motivated by philanthropy or profit. Patented cures, making widely exaggerated, not to say fraudulent, claims as to their efficacy, were advertised with such tedious regularity that intending passengers could be forgiven for feeling nauseous long before they stepped on board ship at all. In reality, the only way to deal with the problem was to endure it.

While the vast majority of passengers would experience seasickness to varying degrees at some part of the voyage, most grew accustomed to the motion of the sea within a few days. By this time the smell in the 'tween decks would have become a problem in itself. There were no sanitation facilities available, especially in bad weather. Chamber pots were supplied but not nearly enough. The only toilets were on deck, to which the passengers had no access in bad weather. It was impossible to maintain any degree of modesty or privacy in such circumstances. It was one of the great ironies of steerage emigration that the worse the conditions, the less that could be done to alleviate the suffering. In fine weather, life in the hold was tolerable because the hatches would be open and a certain amount of access to the deck was allowed. This, if the master and crew were inclined to comply with the law, presented an opportunity to have the steerage accommodation completely washed down. Such inclination, however, was not ever-present and on those occasions when the regulation was enforced the passengers were made do the cleaning themselves in many cases. But in bad weather, when sickness was most widespread, there was no access to fresh air and the hatches were kept firmly battened down. The only relief from the stench were the thick fumes which emanated from surreptitiously smoked pipes. In many instances, the pipe bowls did not contain tobacco but tea leaves. When many of the emigrants were given their ration of tea they did not know what it was. Their normal drink would have been buttermilk. With a commendable waste-not-want-not attitude, they used it to eke out whatever supply of tobacco they might have had. Three hundred and seventeen passengers suffered these conditions in the hold of the *Dunbrody*.[2]

One week into the voyage and the routine had asserted itself. To people on board the *Dunbrody* who had no idea of the distance to be covered, it must have seemed that they would never reach Canada. Finally, after 40 days at sea, there appeared on the distant horizon the faint thickness of shadow which slowly congealed into the unmistakable shape of a distant shore.

Chapter 7

QUEBEC

From the seaward end, Quebec marks the point where the St Lawrence narrows dramatically. To the first Europeans who came here in the late sixteenth and early seventeenth centuries to trap and trade for furs, it was the ideal location in which to establish a trading post. It was the spot where river boats and canoes could rendezvous with ships that would take their goods to Europe and return with metal tools, weapons and trinkets which were used as trading currency with the native tribes of the Algonquin, Iroquois and Huron. These trappers and traders were French and, in typical European tradition, claimed these 'new lands' for the mother country. Trade was brisk. The demand for pelts in the courts and salons of fashionable Europe was insatiable and by 1663 the small trading post had grown sufficiently in importance to be named the capital of New France.

During the eighteenth century the British and French fought for the colony, both using the Algonquin and Iroquois people as pawns in their power struggle. In 1753, Britain eventually proved victorious. They had won the land but not the allegiance of many of the white residents who were to retain French as their first language and cultural identity.

Overzealous trapping and changing fashions took their toll on the fur trade and timber became the main export. There had been some clearing of the primeval forests which stretched right across the continent but it was piecemeal. Even after Britain took control from France the seemingly inexhaustible supply of timber was not of major interest because, prior to the Napoleonic Wars, Britain got most of the timber she needed from the Baltic states. When this source was cut off, however, she looked to her colonies in the west and so began the lucrative trade on which most Canadian seaports would be built. As this trade grew, it was imperative to populate the growing colony with ambitious young men and women who were prepared to work. This resulted in the two-way trade which saw ships carry timber eastwards and emigrants west.

Nowhere benefited from this constant activity more than Quebec. After all, it was easy to reach from the Atlantic and the St Lawrence offered access into the Great Lakes of Upper Canada. Not everyone ventured far into the interior. Some settled in the environs of the port itself or along the river valley. From the 1820s on, many of the immigrants were Irish who took up whatever work was available – farmers, loggers, builders and general labourers ashore and on the rivers. By 1833, there were 7,000 Irish people in Quebec city out of a population of 30,000, almost one-in-four, and the natural leaders among them became politically active. Those Irish who did stay in and around Quebec fell into three categories. There were the Protestant Irish who would not mix with the French-speaking Quebecois because of religious as well as linguistic differences; there were the Catholic Irish who overcame the linguistic barrier with their co-religionists; and there were the Catholic Irish who decided to remain distinct from the French-speaking Catholics as well as from English-speaking Protestants. It should be said that these social barriers were erected by most cultures and were not the monopoly of the Irish.[1]

The Irish comprised the largest English-speaking ethnic group in Quebec throughout the first part of the nineteenth century. They were more numerous than the English, Scottish, Welsh and Americans combined. It is important to remember that the vast majority of these arrived in Quebec between 1814 and 1844 and were not famine emigrants but people who had been smallholders in Ireland and who wanted to make better lives for themselves and their children. They were well settled in ethnic parishes along the St Lawrence valley by the time the exodus of the destitute was under way. While they were prepared to alleviate the sufferings of those at home by sending money when they could, the wave of impoverishment that was about to wash up on their shores was more than anyone could have foreseen.

On 18 May 1847, the *Dunbrody* approached the end of her ocean voyage. Sickness had struck but not to an excessive extent. Five of the passengers had died at sea. To the bereaved, the deaths were heart-breaking, as all deaths are, but in the cold world of official statistics this 1.6% mortality rate was acceptable.[2] Reaching the Canadian coastline was one thing but reaching the end of their journey was another. After they passed Cape Breton, the Gulf of St Lawrence had to be crossed. Then came the strait the French called Detroit d'Honguedo, guarded to the east by the Île d'Anticosti and to the west by the Peninsule de la Gaspesie. Once clear of the strait, they were into the mouth of the great St Lawrence river. The city of Quebec was still more than 350 miles away but it was not the distance that made the prospect daunting. What was to make this the most terrifying part of the voyage was the quarantine station through which they would have to pass before being allowed to step onto the mainland. They would reach that island station about 30 miles short of the city. It was the portal designed to protect the citizens from disease. It was called Grosse Île.

The island was one of many in the St Lawrence. At one and a half miles long by about half a mile wide, it was larger than

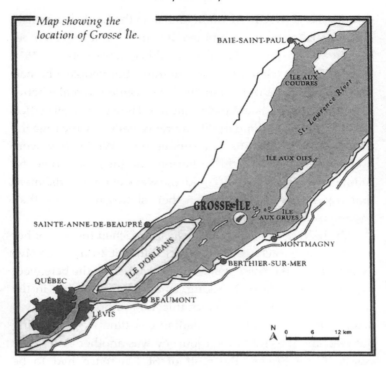

Map showing the location of Grosse Île.

some and smaller than others. It was pretty to look at but its terrain of rocky outcrop and small wooded valleys had little to entice settlers to make a home on it and until 1832 it had been uninhabited. That was the year of widespread and catastrophic cholera outbreaks in England and Ireland. It was feared that emigrants leaving those countries for Canada would carry the disease with them and the authorities ordered a quarantine station established in the St Lawrence to vet new arrivals before they could make their way ashore. Grosse Île fitted the bill. It was near enough to be serviceable and far enough away to be safe. Several sheds were erected on it and they served their purpose satisfactorily until the emergency was passed. Two years later, similar fears caused them to be re-opened. The quarantine station was a reasonable success once again. In 1847, however, it was to prove utterly inadequate.

The man in charge of the station was Dr George Mellis Douglas, a 38-year-old native of Carlisle in the north of England.[3] As well as supervising the station and keeping it maintained, Douglas rented a small farm on the island for which he paid the government $100 a year. He had been appointed to the position in 1837 and his service had gained unstinting praise from all quarters. Secular and religious authorities, as well as independent witnesses, all testified that no better man could be found to run the station. It was not just a job to him. He genuinely cared for the people who passed through the station and his work rate was phenomenal. He was, it was generally believed, a good man to have in a crisis. And a crisis was what they all expected.

From February 1847 news of the potato blight and the resultant starvation in Ireland was given better newspaper coverage in Canada than it was in Britain. Some commentators felt that this arose from the fact that Britain minimised the affects of the potato shortage so that people in Canada and other prospective destinations might not become alarmed at the number and state of destitution of refugees about to land on their shores, while Canadian newspapers felt it their duty to make such knowledge as widely available as possible. Also, as we have seen, the carriage of passengers was supposedly governed by Passenger Acts. Both Britain and the United States had introduced such legislation from time to time. The American measures were far stricter than the British ones. They were not always adhered to but when further restrictions were introduced into law many shipowners felt that the new measures might be enforced more rigorously until such time as the novelty wore off. In March 1847, the US tightened their Passenger Acts in an

Vessels lying at anchor in the quarantine pass off Grosse Île.

effort to stem their tide of pauper immigration. Under these new measures, passengers were entitled to a greater amount of space on board ship and headage payments to the port of entry – a tax for each passenger landed in case they became dependent on public coffers – were to be enforced. This meant fewer passengers could be carried per ship and the headage payments would have to be absorbed by increased fares. To meet the increased costs of complying with the new rules, fares on American ships averaged £5 a head, whereas a ticket on a British vessel going to a port in British North America was seldom, if ever, more than £3-15-0. It was obvious that many poor emigrants who had planned on going to United States would now sail for Canada as an indirect point of entry. Nobody could have predicted the extent to which these observations were to prove true.

The response to the worsening situation was twin-edged. The authorities, dreading the onslaught that was bound to arrive, made some preparation to meet it. As it happened, such preparations were too little, too late. Meanwhile, church leaders and other philanthropists set about raising money which could be sent to Ireland to ease the distress of which they read. Schemes were put forward as to how best to help the destitute Irish. Raising money was the one aspect on which they agreed but it was what to do with the money after it had been raised that caused the difference of opinion. One pragmatist decried the efficacy of sending money to Ireland. Instead, he urged that monies raised could be best used to erect proper facilities in which to receive the immigrants. This made a great deal of sense. Why send money to Ireland when, by the time it reached the poor there, many of them would already be on the Atlantic bound for the very ports from which the money had been sent? What they wanted after the harrowing voyage was good food and shelter and, if funds allowed, a small stake to help them on to their final destinations. Also, the health of the people already resident along the St Lawrence would be safeguarded. In short, money sent to Ireland would be lost whilst money used to good effect in Canada would benefit both the locals and the new arrivals. As spring became summer and Grosse Île sank into the depths of despair, sickness and death, the wisdom of this idea would become all too clear.

Most people were undecided in which way the money should be spent. All they knew was they had to do something. In April 1847, the Emigrant Settlement Association was established in Toronto. Its main purpose was to help immigrants get shelter and work until they could make their own way. In the city of Quebec, the Catholic bishop launched an appeal that raised in excess of £3,000. Those who could give even a little did so, those who lived in the hinterland, in a virtually cashless society, sold produce in the population centres to raise money which they donated to the various funds.

The ice which had closed the St Lawrence to navigation in the long winter months began to recede in late April. Dr Douglas was instructed to have the hospital sheds on Grosse

Île ready for the reception of the first arrivals of the new spring. This he did, having 50 new iron beds installed and a large quantity of straw for those who would have to sleep on the floor. The five sheds could accommodate up to 200 patients and these were to be cared for by a staff of four – Douglas, one steward, one orderly and one nurse. It was the same number which had dealt with the influx of previous years. All was ready by 4 May and ten days later the first emigrant ship of the season arrived. This was the *Syria*, 46 days out of Liverpool. Of her 254 passengers, nine had died during the voyage and more than half (125) of the remaining 245 were ill from the general malaise known as 'ship fever'. Within 24 hours, the first death at Grosse Île in 1847 was recorded.

Douglas immediately recognised the fever as typhus. Fever, headache, listlessness, skin rash, enlargement of liver and spleen, intense thirst and lack of appetite were classic symptoms.[4] He knew, too, that many of the passengers who appeared healthy would show the same symptoms in a week or even less. The disease had an incubation period of seven to ten days after which the first signs of the ailment would make themselves apparent. On about the fifth day a rash would break out and then delirium, culminating in a fixed, vacant stare. The most disheartening aspect was there was little or nothing he could do. Like all fevers, typhus had to take its course. It was his job to help the afflicted as best he could and stop it from spreading. Yet, how was he to curb such contagion? Separate the well from the sick? Detain the latter until they were of no threat to the people of Quebec? Who, apart from the obvious, were 'the sick'? These people had just spent weeks together in fetid, cramped conditions. The 'well' could be dead inside two weeks, contaminating anyone who came in contact with them in the meantime.

Douglas had three days to get his newly-arrived patients organised before the next ship came upriver to anchor off

Grosse Île. The day after that another came, and the day after that another. Two arrived on 19 May, another one on 20 May and five on 21 May. Already there were over 3,000 passengers landed or waiting on board the ships anchored in the roads. The sheds were overcrowded and the small staff impossibly overworked. In the six days since the arrival of the *Syria*, another 40 of her passengers had died in the quarantine hospital. Douglas wrote to the Governor General requesting more accommodation and more staff. Apart from the sick on the island, there were more still on board the ships because there was nowhere to shelter them ashore. Conditions on board those vessels were worse than they had been during the voyage because at sea fresh breezes could be funnelled down to the passengers cooped-up in the holds, but lying at anchor in the river, the breeze was not enough to make it worthwhile. Soon, the shipboard sick started dying as well. On 20 May, 52 people were buried. The following day, another 59 followed suit. The nightmare was only beginning for on the next day, 22 May, a flotilla of fifteen emigrant ships carrying another 3,600 steerage passengers approached Grosse Île. One of these ships was the *Dunbrody*.

Of her passenger complement of 317, five had died at sea and six more were ill with fever as the ship came to rest. Two doctors had arrived on the island and offered their services in the past few days. This left Douglas free to concentrate on boarding the ships to identify the fever victims. They would have to be treated there until more accommodation was available on the island. In most cases, however, they were simply left to fare as best they could until they could be hospitalised ashore. Because of the relatively small incidence of death and illness on board, the *Dunbrody* was cleared from quarantine after three days and no more of her passengers died either on board or on Grosse Île. Compared to the *Scotland*, which had arrived at the island on the same day, the *Dunbrody* had not fared too badly. The *Scotland* had sailed from Cork and had been at sea for 40 days, exactly the same length of voyage as the *Dunbrody* but of her passenger complement of 564, 60 had died at sea and 160 arrived suffering from fever. She was quarantined for sixteen days, during which time 34 more of her passengers died on board and 72 died in the hospitals. This made a total of 166 deaths, about one-in-three of her total number of passengers.

The Emigration Officer at Quebec was Alexander Buchanan, an Irishman who had been born in Omagh, County Tyrone 39 years previously. It was his responsibility to see that the Passenger Acts were observed and that immigrants received all the help they needed on arrival. He pointed out to Douglas that it was a breach of the regulations to leave healthy immigrants on board the ships in close confinement with the ill and they were to be removed to the island immediately. Douglas replied that such a proposal could not be carried out because all the accommodation on Grosse Île was occupied by the sick who had been landed. Where was he to put the healthy? One of the suggestions was to put them on neighbouring Cliff Island but the terrain was unsuitable for tents and the idea was scrapped. The order was given for more accommodation to be erected without delay. The allocation of medical and support staff was also increased. One of the doctors already on the island was 45-year-old John Benson from Castlecomer in County Kilkenny. He had sailed from Ireland on the *Wandsworth* from Dublin, arriving at Grosse Île on 19 May after 42 days. Of her 527 passengers, 51 had died during the voyage and another 78 had fever on arrival. Doctor Benson was one of the healthy ones. Whether from a deep sense of gratitude for his deliverance or of duty to his hypocratic oath, he immediately offered his services to Douglas who assigned him to treating those in the hospital. Benson did not shrink from the task. His bravery cost him his life. He died of the contagion exactly a week after his arrival. On the day of his death, 26 May, 30 vessels lay at anchor, 10,000 passengers waited to be inspected and their immediate fate decided. These inspections were to give rise to several complaints. Firstly, the doctor might not visit a ship for two or three days after arrival and, secondly, the nature of the inspection was so superficial as to strip it of all medical significance.[5]

By 28 May, there were 856 cases of fever and dysentery in the sheds and hospitals, more than four times what Douglas and his staff had been told to cater for a month previously. Out in the river, on board ships which had been inspected, were another 470 cases. Also in the roads were a further 36 vessels, carrying a total of 13,000 passengers. Most of the staff and volunteers grew weak from fatigue and illness. Douglas pleaded for more resources and when these failed to materialise, he warned the authorities in Quebec to prepare for the reception of sick immigrants in the city and also to alert the authorities in Montreal and further upriver into Ontario. He wrote telling them that accommodation for 2,000 people should be erected in both centres. He was certain that half of the people leaving the island would die en route to their destinations.

At Douglas' request, almost 300 army tents and several marquees arrived. They would have to meet the accommodation needs until more substantial structures could be erected. The problem was the medical and support staff on the island were far too busy to erect the tents themselves and no military detachment had been assigned to set up the canvas hospitals and shelters. It was said that army officers refused to allow their men to remain on the island for fear of contagion. Most of the sick were too weak to put them up. Like Dr Benson, some of those who had been declared healthy stayed on to help at the station. Perhaps most of them had at least one family member in one of the makeshift hospitals. Whatever their reasons for staying, they constituted an additional workforce and they erected four of the marquees with 64 beds in each. Many of the tents left by the military were also erected by them. It must also be recorded, however, that there were cases of terror-stricken families deserting fever-stricken relatives.

There were now 40 vessels in a two-mile stretch of river. Deaths on the island and on board the ships were numbering 50 a day. Many families lost more than one member and sometimes both parents died leaving young children behind them. By the close of the month, there were 100 orphans for whom adoptive families would have to be found. The Francophone people of Quebec were unstinting in their generosity to the Irish of Grosse Île. The vast majority of priests and nuns who worked so courageously throughout that summer and autumn were French-Canadians. The people throughout the province gave what they could to ease the suffering on the island. When it came to taking young Irish orphans into their families, they were no less caring and kind-hearted.

In early June, building continued at a frantic pace. Sheds and hospitals were erected on site. Others were prefabricated in Quebec city and shipped downriver for assembly on the island. Douglas lashed out at what he regarded as exaggerated newspaper reports of the conditions on the island. He particularly discounted the reported level of fever cases. Dysentery, he claimed, was by far the most common ailment on Grosse Île. He admitted, however, that the situation was dire and he called for the Passenger Acts to be further tightened to stop Irish landlords sending out people who had neither the physical strength nor financial support to meet the harrowing challenges of an Atlantic crossing.

One thing had been resolved. On 3 June, it was decided to allow the healthy to occupy a portion on the east side of the island. Contact between them and the sick was blocked by a contingent of 50 soldiers who had been sent there at the request of Douglas. This had been a regular precaution to maintain order in previous years. Nevertheless, the conditions on board the ships in the roads continued to deteriorate. Things were so bad that one of the Catholic priests on the island wrote that it would be better if the ships were sunk by cannon fire to save the unfortunate people on board from suffering the slow, agonising deaths which faced so many of them.[6]

Into this living death came the *Erin*. She had left New Ross 54 days earlier, on 12 April, the same day as the *Dunbrody*. Although she had taken two weeks longer to complete the same voyage, it had not been the nightmare experienced by thousands of others who had anchored at Grosse Île in the past few days. Of her 120 passengers only two had died at sea and there was no sign of illness among the rest. As there was no sickness, there was little reason to delay the ship further. In common with all new arrivals, the healthy passengers of the *Erin* were put on the east end of Grosse Île where they were to spend ten days in quarantine. The ship was allowed to proceed to Quebec city on 6 June. Only one more of her passengers died during that ten-day period. At the end of their quarantine, the healthy were then put on board steamers that would take them to Quebec city or further on to Montreal.

This evacuation of the fit was necessary not just to remove them from possible contagion, but also to make room on the island for new arrivals. By the end of the first week of June, thousands were being forwarded to the cities and fears were voiced that many of them were not as healthy as the doctors on Grosse Île diagnosed. Douglas responded vehemently at this slur on his reputation. He pointed out that no one could tell if a person was in the incubatory period of typhus and neither he nor his staff could be held responsible if people arrived in the cities showing symptoms of the disease. Those symptoms could have developed after that person had been released from the island. While this was a sound point, the small staff on Grosse Île caring for the sick and dying, inspecting new arrivals and periodically checking those in the shanty-town of the 'healthy', could not possibly guarantee that no sick people slipped through the net. That same week it was recorded that the death rate of the sick on board the ships was twice that of the hospitalised and three-to-ten times greater than the death rate at sea. In those fetid, repulsive 'tween decks, the sick lay with the dead. Complaints of the stench surrounding the island and its fleet of disease-ridden brigs and barques were becoming louder and more frequent. On 9 June, the *Standard* arrived.

She had slipped away from the quay at New Ross on 21 April and took 49 days to reach the station. Of her 369 passengers (four of whom were in cabins), six had died en route and another twelve were sick on arrival. The ship was to remain where she was for ten days, during which time four more died. Two of the ill who were removed to one of the hospitals died some time later.

Over the next two weeks, much was done to house all the sick on the western part of the island, as well as all the healthy immigrants on the eastern side. Nevertheless, by the time the next ship out of New Ross, the *Progress*, arrived on 26 June, not all the passengers could leave the ship without delay. She was detained in quarantine for eighteen days because during her 52 days at sea there had been 27 deaths and 68 cases of sickness when she dropped anchor. Another 31 were to die in hospital and five on board the ship during the quarantine period.

The following day, six more ships arrived with 2,033 passengers. Three of these had left New Ross. The *John Bell*, 47 days out, had no cases of illness but had lost seven of her 254 passengers en route. The *Agent* had been 39 days at sea and had lost eight of her 387 passengers during the voyage and four more were to die in hospital while a fifth died on board during her four-day quarantine.

The *Solway* had a relatively fast crossing of 30 days. Three of her 364 passengers had died at sea and two were sick on arrival. The day after that, 28 June, yet another ship from New Ross arrived. The *Margaret*, Captain J. Black, had been 40 days at sea and ten of her 531 passengers had died en route, of her twenty sick eleven were to die in hospital and a further five on board the ship during her four days in quarantine. Two days later, the *Margrette*, Captain Hardcastle, sailed in with another 399 passengers, 59 days out of New Ross. She had fourteen cases of sickness and 21 passengers had died at sea. Unfortunately, it is not possible to say how many of the passengers on board these ex-New Ross ships were from the Fitzwilliam estate but the *Dunbrody, Solway, Agent* and others yet to be mentioned have been identified as ships used in the clearance of the estate. Also references to ships used appear in various documents in the Fitzwilliam Papers but only some of the tenants/emigrants in 1847 can be positively matched with the name of the ships on which they sailed.

By mid-June, the situation on the island had become intolerable for all those trapped on it by circumstance or duty. Letters of the clergy to their bishops (both Catholic and Anglican) reflect this. The sick died, the well became ill, the priests, nuns, doctors, nurses, and volunteers seemed to contract either the fever or dysentery with appalling regularity. On average, a new helper or member of staff fell ill after just eighteen to 21 days.[7] And still worse was to come. Towards the end of the third week in June the sky clouded over and drops began to fall. It rained for a week, turning the earth to mud and churning the mud into a morass. The soiled and dirty bed clothes could not be washed or dried and the filthy blankets accumulated adding to the pervasive stench which now hung over Grosse Île. Those who had been sleeping in the open on the bare ground now found their resting places to be mire. The heavy rain

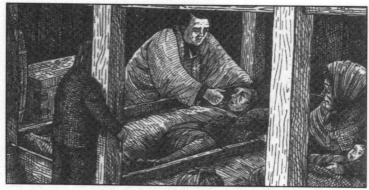

A Catholic priest administers the Last Rites to a dying man in steerage quarters on an emigrant ship in Grosse Île.

tore at the shallow graves and the rivulets which flowed from them carried the corrupted fluids of the corpses to the open drain which ran between the rows of tents. Then the rain stopped. It had impeded the burial parties and when it ceased, interments recommenced. Because of the underlying rock, many of the graves were no more than three feet deep. These attracted the ship rats to the island to gnaw at the bodies. To counteract this, soil was dug from the small hillocks and put on the graves. Six men were detailed to burying the dead, a task at which they were constantly employed.

Throughout the summer, boats of all shapes and sizes, some of sail and some of steam, plied the river. They operated between the mainland and the ships, the ships and the island, the island and the mainland. They carried supplies, they ferried those who appeared well to Quebec, they ferried those who appeared ill to the hospital. Yet, despite all this water-borne activity, the parish priest of Sherbrooke, Fr Bernard O'Reilly, complained that he could not get anyone to ferry him out to the ships where passengers were dying without the consolation of clergy. He and other clergymen had to rely on the goodwill of members of ships' crews to take them across. While many of the sailors did perform this small act of mercy, many others did not with the result that passengers died on board without receiving the last rites. Nor was this his only complaint. He admired the work of Douglas and his staff but condemned the lack of official support for them. Douglas, he said, was doing the work of three, but not even the superhuman efforts of so few could do anything against such overwhelming odds.

Another priest, Fr William Moylan, deplored the way in which patients were left unattended for up to eighteen hours at a time. He also recorded the way in which the filth of patients in the upper bunks seeped between the boards to drip on those below, reminiscent of life in the hold during the ocean voyage. As well as that, he questioned the integrity of some of the staff and helpers, convinced that theft of money and other possessions from the sick and dying was going on. Douglas admitted that such was the case but was at a loss to know what to do about it. His main concern was to save the lives of the ill, not stand guard over their money.

Douglas himself became the target of accusations. It was said that he used some of the boatmen to work his farm on the island and that he sold its produce to patients for profit. Nothing was proven and the matter was shelved while the crisis continued. The general attitude seems to have been that Douglas' uncontested workrate and dedication to the sick was such that even if he did make money from the farm his good points far outweighed the bad. Nevertheless, a committee was established to enquire into the management of the station.

Only two ships arrived from New Ross in July. The *W.S. Hamilton* arrived on 1 July. Thirty of her 207 passengers were sick, four had died en route, eighteen more were to die in hospital and two more during the six days the ship was kept in quarantine. The *Pandora*, with 401 passengers, dropped anchor on 30 July – twelve had died at sea and 59 were sick. Another

A nurse at work in one of the Quarantine Station hospitals.

nine died in hospital and a further three died on board during the ship's five days in quarantine.

By 16 July, there were 3,500 people on the island, 2,000 of whom were in the hospital sheds. The death rate was between 30 and 40 a day.

Throughout August more and more vessels arrived. As soon as they dropped anchor, the signal requesting the medical officer was hoisted but it could be a day or two before a visit was made. Most of the ships had sailed from England and Ireland. Even those from England carried mostly Irish passengers. There were also ships from Germany. The place of origin of a vessel was immediately recognisable from its appearance. The German ships were neat and tidy, the passengers healthy and robust. Those from Liverpool and the ports of Ireland reeked of disease and death. The clothes which were hung on rigging to dry were as indicative as national flags. The wretched rags on most signified Irish passengers.[8] As a well-known cartoon of the time depicted them, they were floating poorhouses. One example was the *Virginius* from Liverpool. Of her 476 passengers, only 318 survived. The master, mate, steward, and nine of the crew also perished with fever. The remainder of the crew had to rely on the weakened efforts of some of the passengers to complete the voyage.

On 24 August, the *Colonist* furled her sails and came to rest at the station, 43 days out of New Ross. Of her 453 passengers, 30 were sick, of whom thirteen were later to die in hospital. Twelve had been buried at sea. She was the last vessel from New Ross to stop at Grosse Île that year. The *Dunbrody* made a second trip across the Atlantic, arriving in the St Lawrence in September, as did the *Tottenham* and the *George Ramsey*. They carried twelve, five, and eight passengers respectively and there were no cases of sick so were allowed to proceed directly to Quebec city.

September saw a decrease in the number of ships arriving. For several weeks, worries had been voiced about the approaching autumn. None of the sheds on the island had been equipped to withstand the ravages of a Canadian winter. The island population fell as more and more patients were declared fit and sent to Quebec and Montreal in steamers. By 21 September, 1,276 remained. Three days later, the decision was taken to move them to the cities as soon as they became strong enough and before the close of the season. By 23 October, there were none left and preparations to seal the buildings against the severe weather got under way. The capacity of the station had increased eleven-fold since the beginning of the season six months earlier. It could now accommodate 2,300 people. On 3 November, it was officially closed for the winter.

DISPERSAL

The city of Quebec was the gateway west and south. Few of the famine Irish intended staying there. Many of them had entered Canada merely as a cheap route to the United States and, once they hit the mainland, they sought the Old Canada Road, an historic route that would take them across the narrow strip of southern Quebec and into the state of Maine. Once in the US they could seek the cities of the east or the promise of the pioneering west.[9]

Those who had been lucky enough to be considered fit were brought upriver to Quebec and Montreal by steamer. These steamers varied in size from small workboats up to substantial craft which, in happier times, would be put to more agreeable uses. As Douglas had warned, however, appearances were deceptive and many of these people fell ill along the way. Quebec city had a marine hospital which was soon filled to capacity and beyond. Temporary sheds were erected but these, too, proved inadequate. Many of the destitute were delayed here. Some were not destined to complete their journeys. Perhaps it would have been kinder had they died on Grosse Île rather than be so tricked by fate. For those going up to Montreal, the trip was no idyllic river cruise. Alexander Buchanan, the Emigration Officer at the port of Quebec, told the Special Committee which had been set up to enquire into the management of the Quarantine Station at Grosse Île (this was established in July in response to the reports of the horrific conditions on the island) that:

> Those who are healthy, if sent up as hitherto to Montreal, must bring with them the seeds of sickness and become inmates of the sheds, while out of the number who can leave Montreal for a further destination, the large majority are pre-doomed to expire on the wharves of Kingston or Toronto.

He went on to say that bearing in mind the squalid conditions in which these people had crossed the ocean, breathing in contagion, been subjected to poor food and lack of air, they were particularly prone to contracting the disease.

> When they left the station, they were literally crammed on board the steamers, exposed to the cold night air, or the

burning summer's sun, and in this state, the most robust constitution must give way to an unbroken series of hardships. Montreal and the whole Province have learned the consequence of thus allowing Emigrants to leave Grosse Île without a sufficient sanitary probation, as well as the effects of permitting 800, 900, or 1,000 persons in a state of uncleanliness and debility to be huddled for 48 hours together on the deck of a steamboat.[10]

Not surprisingly, some died during the two days it took to complete the 150-mile trip.

Montreal had a population of 44,093 people of whom 15,268 were English, Scottish or Irish. It had the trappings of civilization. Its 23 colleges, academies and convents, its 68 elementary schools, its cricket clubs and other centres of gentlemanly leisure all gave testimony to the high regard in which the citizenry held their city and themselves. The expected flood of destitute and disease-bearing immigrants caused widespread fear in this fine city and it was decided that shelters should be erected along the waterfront, away from the populated areas. At Pointe St Charles, three sheds were put up as temporary hospitals for they knew, even before the ships began to arrive, that Grosse Île would not be able to cope with the demands that were to be placed upon it. Douglas' warning of sick immigrants 'getting through' was well heeded and even anticipated. When the onslaught came more sheds were built until there were 22 in all. The stench of sickness and death hung over the shanty town as it did at Grosse Île. The weather grew warmer until in June it was said to be 'a summer of Calcutta heat'.[11]

One of the convents in the city was that of the Grey Nuns. They heard the stories of the Irish immigrants by the river. Among the rumours was the story that the sick, dying and dead all lay together. Few had either the strength or the will to bury the corpses. Indeed, the sick did not seem to care if they were the next to die. Whatever spirit they might once have had had deserted them. The stories seemed too horrifying to be true. Mother McMullen, the convent Superior, asked Sr Sainte-Croix to accompany her to the river so that she might see the state of the immigrants for herself. Nothing prepared her for what she saw. Plucking up their courage, both nuns entered the sheds and experienced that potent surge of revulsion, anger, and compassion that galvanise the strong to action.

Mother McMullen requested the Emigration Officer to allow her to work with the sick. He was only too happy to secure her help and told her to do what she deemed necessary. Such a dangerous task would have to be taken on by volunteers. She could not command her nuns to follow her into such danger. Consequently, she called them together, explained the situation and reminded them of their vows of sacrifice in the service of their faith.[12] Forty of the sisters volunteered.

Shifts were organised and the nuns went to work. By the end of their first week in the sheds, on 24 June, the first signs that two of their number had contracted the fever appeared. One by one, others became victims and within a short space of time, 30 of the 40 nuns were seriously ill, some of them dying. The Sisters of Providence, hearing of the stricken nuns, sent replacements to look after them and the other patients in the hospital sheds. Over the next few weeks, seven of the Grey Nuns died. The others recuperated and, by September, they were back in force tending to the sick. As at Grosse Île, priests, Anglican and Catholic, were also to the fore. They were joined by Jesuits sent up from Fordham in New York. Other helpers included Captain Hammond of the local garrison and a retired Royal Navy man, Lt Lloyd, who became one of those to die because of their work in the sheds.

Not everyone showed such compassion. Many citizens demanded that the immigrants not be allowed to land in

Montreal but to keep them moving on to Toronto – or anywhere. Mass protest meetings were held on the Champ de Mars and rumours circulated that there was a band of militants who proposed to march on the shanty town and throw the sheds and shelters into the river. One restraining voice in all this was the mayor, John Easton Mills. Not only did he defuse the situation, but he volunteered to work in the hospitals. He did not hide behind his office nor was the offer a political stunt. Mills went into the worst of the

Celtic High Cross erected by the Anceint Order of Hibernians on Grosse Île, 1909, in memory of the Irish who died fleeing the famine.

sheds and worked side-by-side with the other helpers. He caught the fever and died on 12 November.

Of course, many of the patients also died. Hundreds of children were left parentless. The Grey Nuns took charge of these orphans and the bishop, Msgr Ignace Bourget, circulated an appeal for families to adopt one or two of these unfortunate children. The response was overwhelming and soon all the children were placed in new homes. As had happened in Quebec, many of the host families were Francophone and the children were raised in the Acadian tradition.

Kingston and other centres along the river were to experience the influx of famine Irish over that and subsequent summers. Toronto fared better than Quebec and Montreal, merely because it was further on and fewer of the sick reached it.

STATISTICS

In a crisis of such magnitude, the accuracy of record-keeping can, understandably, take second place to the immediate work in hand. This can lead to confusing and contradictory statistics. According to Marianna O'Gallagher and Rose Masson Dompierre in their book *Eyewitness – Grosse Île 1847*:

> The authorities at Grosse Île and in Quebec furnished precise figures as to the characteristics of the immigration of 1847. Roughly we may summarise them here: 98,000 people, of whom 6,110 had been given 'assisted passage', embarked on 442 vessels in the different ports of Europe for the port of Quebec. The 1847 immigration was made up of 78,700 Irish, 8,500 English, 7,400 Germans and 3,700 Scots. Of that number 4,100 died at sea; 8,150 in the different hospitals in Quebec and Ontario; and 5,424 were buried at the Quarantine Station at Grosse Île. The vast majority of those deaths occurred among the Irish. The survivors eventually established themselves in Canada and the United States, and contributed to the building of North American society.

The death rate was one-in-eight. Among those statistics of living and dead are the people who had left the Fitzwilliam estate.

THE PROGRAMME PROCEEDS

By the end of 1847, the names of 313 families consisting of 2,207 individuals had been entered in the Coolattin estate Emigration Book. Although some families were delayed and their names appear in the following year's register as well, the vast majority of those scheduled to go that year had left the estate for Quebec as arranged. Many of these were destined for Ontario, but some probably made their way further south into the United States. The horrors of Grosse Île shortened the journeys of several and some of these can be identified by comparing the lists of the dead at the quarantine station with the Emigration Books in the Fitzwilliam Papers. No doubt, as Dr Douglas had warned, many did not survive long after leaving Grosse Île. Those who did survive moved into the vast wooded areas west of Kingston or down into the south-west peninsula which separated Lake Erie from Lake Huron.

Back on the Coolattin estate, plans to continue the clearance programme were well in hand. As the new year was ushered in, the speculation which had gripped the tenants the previous year was no doubt repeated. By March, more names were entered for emigration. The register which had been used twelve months earlier was full and a new one was opened.[13] Once again, William Graves was contracted to supply the ships and Phase Two got under way. Despite the horror stories of Grosse Île, Quebec was once more the destination for all the Fitzwilliam tenants emigrating that year – all, that is, except for one shipload that was bound for a small port in south-west New Brunswick. The years subsequent to 1847 saw some improvement in the conditions at Grosse Île and nothing was to compare with Black '47 on the island. Experience and greater preparation combined to make the station more efficient.

Chapter 8

NEW BRUNSWICK

The province of New Brunswick was a not a favoured destination for emigrants until the timber trade had begun to clear tracts along the edges of the dense forests. Even then the numbers of European settlers were quite insignificant. As the nineteenth century dawned, however, they began arriving in increasing, but still unspectacular, numbers and it was not until the economic depression in Europe during the post-Napoleonic years that the province really began to open up.

For the most part, these settlers were Protestants who had a little capital with which to establish themselves. By the time the famine refugees arrived there was already a strong Irish presence in the province but apart from their country of origin there was little in common between the earlier immigrants and the new wave. The new arrivals were mostly Catholic and lacked the wherewithal to carve out new lives for themselves. Most simply saw New Brunswick as a landing point from which to venture west, either to Upper Canada (present day Ontario) or the United States. Some had no option but to stay, trapped by poverty. These trends are reflected in the fact that the great majority of today's New Brunswick-Irish are descended from pre-famine emigrants.

In the south-west corner of the province is the small town of St Andrews. It is a picturesque town, clean and well-proportioned.

The residents obviously take a pride in their community and tourists flock there in the summer months. Half of its houses and stores are over 100 years old. Some are older and a few date back to the town's origins in 1783. A venerated two or three pre-date the town itself. This rather strange phenomenon is easily explained.

When victory for George Washington's revolutionary army was assured, many loyalists in the American colonies felt they could not live as 'Americans' and, to preserve their British identity, they moved to Canada. These were known as the United Empire Loyalists. UELs in the state of Maine simply crossed the Ste Croix river into New Brunswick. Several of them rafted their houses across and re-erected them in their chosen locations. One of the towns they established was St Andrews. As if re-location were not sufficient evidence of their loyalty, they named the streets King, Queen, Princess Royal and Prince of Wales. Other streets were dedicated to British political and military figures. It was a British town for British people.

The site was well chosen. Perched on a headland in Passamaquoddy Bay, it had all-year access to the sea which teemed with fish stocks and the well-wooded hinterland promised land-based wealth. It was the timber supplies which were to prove the more lucrative. The war between Britain and Napoleonic France cut off Britain's European timber sources in the Baltic. The government looked to the Maritime Provinces of British North America for replacements and small ports like St Andrews embarked on a sustained period of relative prosperity. By the 1830s, however, fortunes had taken a downturn. The demand for timber and for the dried fish which St Andrews exported to the West Indies fell steadily. Also, several changes in British trade policy with the United States and various internal factors, such as the creation of rival designated outports in the vicinity, eroded St Andrews' position as the principal trading port in the region. Local businessmen realised that something would have to be done if St Andrews was to survive. As a port, it still had a great deal going for it and they hit upon the idea of making it the winter port of Quebec and, consequently, of all points south and west of the St Lawrence. After all, the St Lawrence was frozen for several months of the year, greatly curtailing the trade of the Lower and Upper Canadas. If a rail link could be constructed between St Andrews and Quebec city such trade would have all-year access to the Atlantic. It was a proposal worth pursuing.

In 1835 a public meeting was held in the town and support for the project was such that the St Andrews & Quebec Railway Association came into being. It was clear from the outset that the Association meant business and within a year plans were submitted to the New Brunswick Legislative Assembly for ratification. Again, it found widespread support. Seeing the wider benefits of the project, the government of neighbouring Nova Scotia also backed the scheme as, more predictably, did the government of Quebec. The Association commissioned a survey of the route as far as the New Brunswick–Quebec border. But enthusiasm was not enough. Financial backing had to be secured if the ambitious plans were to come to fruition. A delegation was dispatched to London to do just that and the British government granted £10,000 towards the costs of the survey. The New Brunswick Legislative Assembly passed a bill incorporating the railroad company with a capital stock of £750,000 and construction could begin when one-third of the shares had been subscribed.[1]

The company and the general populace could have been forgiven for thinking that everything was moving along nicely and that work would soon begin on this life-line for the region but it was not to be. Interests in the state of Maine, across the international border, claimed that the proposed line would run through US territory which New Brunswick had no right to allocate. They made their protest to the British Colonial Office who ordered work on the survey to halt until the matter had been sorted out. Boundary disputes are notoriously difficult to resolve and for eight years the project was put on hold.

Despite a temporary improvement in timber exports in the first half of the 1840s, those years had not been good for St Andrews' long-term prospects. By the time the dispute was settled in 1842 the railroad was more important to the town than ever. But even settlement of the claims and counter-claims created a problem. The newly-defined boundary was farther east than had been originally accepted with the result that if the St Andrews–Quebec railroad was to remain exclusively within

Canadian territory the route would have to be altered, adding greatly to its anticipated length. This, of course, necessitated revision of estimated costs. It took another three years to get the scheme back on the starting blocks.

In October 1845, a new committee was formed to re-activate the project. Delegates were sent to neighbouring provinces and across the Atlantic to England. As shares were subscribed even greater efforts were made to increase the number of investors. In the summer of 1847, Moses Perley and Captain Robinson visited London where they were successful in disposing of 'a large amount of stock'. They also formed a board of influential shareholders of which Lord Fitzwilliam was appointed president.[2] Ironically, this was just about the time when the first of Fitzwilliam's emigrant tenants reached Grosse Île.

The Legislative Assembly passed the appropriate Bill granting property rights and building materials to the company as well as agreeing to underwrite a guaranteed minimum dividend of 5% (to the English investors only) for a period of ten years. Everything was in place and work began on the long-awaited railroad in November 1847.

Back on the Coolattin estate, Robert Challoner was already thinking about the new phase of clearances.

Fitzwilliam was aware that the need to continue his estate clearance programme and the need for a large unskilled workforce on the railroad project could be mutually addressed. In February 1848, three months after the initial work of clearing and levelling the proposed route had begun, and just as Robert Challoner was getting ready to ship that year's quota of 'surplus tenantry' off the estate, it was agreed between Fitzwilliam and the railroad directors that he would supply 100 men for three months at the rate of two shillings a day – which was double a labourer's daily wage in Ireland.[3] Fitzwilliam would underwrite the wage costs involved – about £1,000 – and, in return, would receive an appropriate amount of shares in the company. However, within the wording of this agreement lay the seeds of a misunderstanding which was to have catastrophic effects in the months ahead. Challoner set about organising not only 100 able-bodied men but also the families of those men, comprising over 380 individuals to emigrate to St Andrews. On 6 March, he wrote to Messrs Graves of New Ross:

> Sirs, It is Lord Fitzwilliam's intention to emigrate 100 families to St Andrews, New Brunswick. I should be glad to have a proposal from you for their passage.[4]

Although Challoner specifically refers to 100 families in the letter, it appears from the passenger list and other sources that the total number of families was 55.[5] Several of the families had two or more able-bodied men, so the 100-strong workforce would not necessarily mean 100 different families.

There is no record of Graves' reply but it must have met with the approval of the estate for he was contracted to charter a ship for the voyage. In the meantime, Challoner set about informing the families he wished to clear.

The pattern of clearance that had been set the previous year was continued. The emigration ledger had been filled with the names of those leaving the estate in 1847 and a new one had to be opened.[6] The number of families to be 'cleared' in the new year was half the 1847 total. It amounted to 181 families, comprising 1,271 individuals and, as in the previous year, they came from all over the south-west corner of County Wicklow. Most were destined for Quebec.

As this was taking place, William Graves secured the services of the *Star*. According to an advertisement he later inserted in the local newspaper, this was a fully-rigged ship of 1,150 tons. In common with most, if not all, ship brokers of the time, Graves had a tendency to exaggerate the size of the ships he used. In general, his advertised tonnages were almost double that shown in Lloyd's Register. The *Star* which entered New Ross on 3 April 1848 was recorded as 727 tons, arriving in ballast from Liverpool.[7] She was locally owned, probably by Graves himself, and was undoubtedly the *Star* in question. At such a tonnage, she was still a good-sized vessel for the time.

Challoner's – and, presumably, Fitzwilliam's – concern for the tenants' welfare en route is evident from a letter he wrote to Graves on 4 April requesting a report from the medical attendant of the *Star* before the ship sailed and to have another report on the state of the passengers on their arrival at St Andrews. He also wanted an account of any deaths that may have taken place, giving the name and previous residence of the deceased. This was agreed to.[8] The *Star* sailed on 21 April (some sources say 18 April) and exactly a week later Challoner informed Graves that the next Canada-bound vessel could be engaged. This time the destination was to be Quebec. This reversion to Quebec would indicate that the supply of labourers to St Andrews had been intended as a once-off agreement. This, in the light of subsequent events, was just as well.

In the case of the *Star*, the crossing was to prove too much for four of the adults and five of the children. According to the *Wexford Independent*, Captain Baldwin, the ship's master, had a good reputation and the passengers were later to give him credit for acting laudably throughout the voyage. He adhered to the latest requirements of the Passenger Act, seeing to it that the ship was cleansed, fumigated and ventilated at regular intervals and there was no apparent cutting back on provisions. The weather had been favourable until they reached the Banks, when the seas rose up around the ship and the relentless pitching and tossing took its toll as the passengers were forced to remain below.

Because of the number of passengers she carried, the *Star*'s complement list included a surgeon. Even if he was conscientious, there was little he could do to alleviate the suffering in steerage. His power to cure would have been greatly restricted and his inclination to tend would depend on his own health as much as on his character. Of the 383 passengers, 63 were badly stricken, nine of whom died.[9] One poor soul was born en route, only to die ten days later. By the time they reached St Andrews on 28 May after 37 days at sea, they no doubt believed that the worst was behind them.

Passamaquoddy Bay has a sprinkling of islands and the *Star* came to anchor off the most wretched of these. Its proper name was Little Hardwood Island but was better known as Hospital Island for it was here that the immigrants would have to be inspected before they would be allowed to step onto the mainland. It was a miserable lump of reddish sand held together by grassy tufts. It measured three acres and looked as if it had dropped unceremoniously from the sky, plopping into the bay three-and-a-half miles north east of St Andrews. Unlike the bigger Hardwood Island, a few hundred yards to the east, Hospital Island had no well or spring. Water had to be ferried across the sound between the two islands. Like Grosse Île in Quebec, it had been designated a quarantine station in 1832, in response to the arrival of cholera and typhus sufferers and had been chosen because it was the least valuable piece of property in the bay. A hospital, measuring 60 feet by 25 feet, of two storeys and a basement, was erected to cope with the emergency. Another smaller one (50 feet by 25 feet), was added later as were a doctor's house, a keeper's house and a shed. Bad as the cholera scare had been, the inadequacy of the island's facilities really came to light fifteen years later, in Black '47. Famine-stricken emigrants sailed in on dilapidated ships with greater frequency than had been experienced before. Dr Samuel Frye, the Medical Officer in St Andrews at that time, echoed the cries of Dr Douglas at

Grosse Île when he wrote to the magistrates pleading for more funds and more facilities. Frye was a successful and compassionate man, one who took his hypocratic oath seriously. He tended the sick and dying but, before his pleas for more support were answered, he contracted typhus fever and died. Other medical and general staff were found to tend the sick but the loss of Frye was a severe blow.

It was a year after his death that the *Star* dropped anchor off the island. Much as the passengers and crew would have liked to leave the ship immediately, they could not do so until they had been inspected by the port's Medical Officer. The overall welfare of arriving immigrants, however, was the responsibility of the port's Acting Emigration Officer.

Until the previous year, there had been one Emigration Officer for the province. He was Moses Perley who was based at St John. This was the same Moses Perley who was so active in raising funds for the proposed railway. The influx of famine refugees, however, made it imperative that other ports should also be adequately supervised by new appointees. James Boyd was appointed Acting Emigration Officer at St Andrews. His appointment had not been unanimously welcomed and local politics were to lead to disgraceful bickering.

In the company of Dr McStay, Boyd visited the *Star* the day after she arrived and spoke to the passengers to see if they had any complaints about their treatment at the hands of the captain and crew on the voyage. They 'all spoke unequivocally in the highest terms of the master and the surgeon'.[10] Boyd reported that the sick should be immediately landed on Hospital Island and the ship sent to Quarantine Island for at least ten days.[11] Half the well passengers were to be landed, the rest were to wash and clean on board before moving to the island for a few days prior to final discharge. The reason for this splitting of the passengers into two groups was because there was not room to accommodate them all on Hospital Island at the one time.

Boyd ordered the master of the *Star* to send on shore any provisions that had been designated for the use of the emigrants. In contradiction to the glowing reports he had heard from the passengers about their treatment and the provisions during the voyage, the quality of the food Baldwin unloaded was so poor that many deemed it unsafe to eat. Complaints were made to Boyd daily by the emigrants and others of the overcrowded conditions. In desperation, they asked that they be distributed along the railway line for the purpose of working but this was not possible as the railway company had not yet erected shanties for them.

Incensed at this neglect, Boyd called on Harris Hatch, the Vice-President of the Company, and described to him the wretched situation of these people where between 200 and 300 were crowded into places not sufficient to contain a third of that number. Many of them lay on a little straw to insulate them from the bare ground. Hatch told him to mind his own business. But, as Acting Emigration Officer, the welfare of the emigrants was Boyd's business. The railway company, however, felt that once they had been landed, he no longer had any authority in the matter. Boyd was not so easily dismissed and he warned that if the company did not supply 'proper wholesome provision and furnish them with more accommodation', he would feel it his duty to do so and report the conduct of the company to the Lieutenant Governor.[12] This had the desired effect and work on building shanty accommodation got under way. Primitive though they were, had the shanties been ready when the ship arrived Boyd was sure that much of the post-arrival sickness would have been avoided. Because of this negligence and the refusal of the company to look after those who became sick and required medical attention, Boyd felt that the company and not the province should be made pay the expenses.

Boyd, it would appear at first glance, was indisputably in charge of the situation but such was not the case. The doctor whom he had taken on board the ship, McStay, was not the port's official Medical Officer and on the same day that Boyd wrote his report on the *Star* to John S. Saunders, the Provincial Secretary, Dr Edwin Bayard, who was the St Andrews Medical Officer, wrote a letter of complaint to the local magistrates.

Saint Andrews, 29 May, 1848

Gentlemen,

I beg to state that, acting under your instruction of the 29th inst. I was this morning preparing to proceed to Quarantine Island to attend to the landing of the passengers from the ship *Star*, Capt Baldwin, from New Ross, ... when I met James Boyd Esq. who stated that I had nothing to do with the Passengers after the ship has been ordered to the Quarantine ground. That he having been appointed Emigrant Officer then took charge of them, and had the power to appoint a Medical Officer and had appointed A. McStay, who has accompanied him to the Island. He states also that the Magistrates had no more to do with the matter.[13]

The passengers of the *Star* could not have cared less about this squabble. They had endured a bad ocean crossing and many were extremely ill. On 2 June, Boyd again wrote to John Saunders, with distressing news. It had rained every day since the arrival of the *Star*, making conditions on the island even worse than usual. In that time there had been six new cases (presumably of fever) resulting in four deaths – one adult and three children ranging in ages from three to ten years of age. When the weather broke, cleaning and washing got underway and things began to look better. Boyd expressed the hope that a large proportion of the passengers would be released from Quarantine Island and landed on the mainland in the following days, 'as they are a most desperate band to manage. The remainder of the well will be sent to Town, as soon as I can get them in a state fit for leaving. They are very foul in their persons, and it is with much difficulty I can get them to wash. The weather continues very fine and they have every opportunity to do so'. He also said that the directors of the railway company were preparing to receive them as they were discharged.[14]

The bad relations between Boyd and the magistrates developed into a feud in which the passengers of the *Star* were caught in the middle. Even the question of whom should be landed was a bone of contention between them, resulting in Captain Baldwin of the *Star* receiving conflicting orders.

Boyd's disapproval of a general landing was justified when it became obvious that some of those landed on the mainland had been released too quickly and that fever was making its presence felt there. On 8 June, he again reported to Saunders:

> Since my last report, there have been landed, at the place appointed by the Managers of the Railroad, 185 more of the passengers, making in all landed 265 and leaving in Hospital Island 98, 87 of whom are in various stages of sickness, and quite a number of bad cases. With the sick, I left eleven of their relations to assist in taking care of them. There were two more deaths yesterday, making in all up to the 7th eleven deaths.
>
> On my return from the Island yesterday, I visited the place where the passengers were landed, and found seven new cases of sickness. I lost no time in sending a Physician, who on his return reported to me that they were fever cases and ought to be immediately removed to the Island and that from the crowded state of those who are in the charge of the Railroad Company, he was fearful there would be many more cases. I have addressed a note to those Gentlemen, requesting that they would provide more expensive accommodation for them, supply them with a better description of food, and remove the sick to the Island without loss of time, which I presume they will attend to.[17]

One of the new fever sufferers was the doctor who had sailed out on the *Star*. His illness was a double blow in that it not only added to the list of patients but it also reduced the capabilities of an already-overwhelmed medical staff. As patients died, Boyd was presented with an additional dilemma. What was he to do about widows and orphans? The budget with which he had to work was grossly inadequate for the scale of the problems he faced. Nevertheless, he had to find some way of stretching it to care for the bereaved as well as for the afflicted. His letters regularly attest to the need for more funds and how, despite careful husbanding of what was allocated to him, he was constantly overspent.

From the foregoing letters which Boyd sent to the Provincial Secretary, it would appear that he genuinely had the emigrants' welfare at heart. Admittedly, it is difficult to make an unbiased judgement solely from letters written by himself. Nevertheless, if he did all he said he did, no better man could have been appointed to his position. His reference to the island being seven miles from the town must mean a round trip as three-and-a-half miles distance is more accurate.

There were those, however, who were not pleased with his performance and the disagreement between Boyd and the local magistrates as to who had the right to inspect the health of immigrants on arrival continued. On 9 June, the Lieutenant Governor's Office wrote to Boyd informing him that he must co-operate with the magistrates. Four days later he replied:

> I have to acknowledge your letter of the 9th inst. with a copy of the opinion of the Attorney General as to whose right it was to appoint a physician to attend the sick passengers landed from the Ship *Star* by which opinion I shall be guided, and endeavour, as far as in me lies, to co-operate with the Justices of the Town of Saint Andrews in carrying out His Excellency's views; although I am aware I shall find it a difficult task. If these Gentlemen had been activated in the first instance by a desire to perform their

public duties (and I speak advisedly) and not allowed themselves, some from personal pique, some from disappointment at
my being invested with the authority that I have been, no
difficulty would have happened.

I visited the Island on the 8th at which time there were 85
persons under treatment and four sailors belonging to the *Star*.
The Physician reported about 30 are in a convalescent state and
from my own observation the general appearance of the patients
was much for the better. The Widows Furlong, Foley and Byrne I
have removed to the Town and found rooms for them as the
overcrowded state of the Emigrants with their families who are to
be employed on the Railroad would not permit of my leaving
them there unprotected and poorly fed. I again visited the Island
on the 10th and 11th. I have now on the Island altogether upward
of 100 persons to preserve besides the persons hired by me to wait
upon the sick and in charge of the provisions and necessaries,
four in number. I have also the eighteen sick at the Railroad
station with three widows and nineteen children amounting in all
to 149 persons to provide for daily, which draws from me much
ready money.

I have received from the Orphans of David White 40
Shillings Currency, for which I shall hold myself accountable.
Two of my attendants, one of whom I had dismissed, are said to
have taken the fever.

My whole time from early morning till late at night is taken
up in the care and management of these people.[18]

He then added a post-script:

Since my last report there have been four more deaths. Three at
the Island and one at the Railroad station; viz: Anthony Leless
aged 30; Ann White and sister, both orphan children; and
Cochran Doyle, aged 26. At the Railroad station, Thomas
Steadman 55. Steadman died after two days illness.

On the same day that the last quoted letter was written, the
magistrates also wrote to Saunders saying that they were prepared to work with Boyd. They also pointed out that the railway

company was giving food to people who had left Quarantine Island for the mainland but who were too debilitated to work. This was putting a strain on the company's resources and they could not be expected to continue such charitable work for long. By law, the magistrates were required to supply food to immigrants only as long as they remained on the island. To solve this problem, they requested the Provincial Secretary to allow them to take whatever measures were necessary.[19]

Needless to say, the directors of the railway company were far from pleased with the situation. On the one hand, they were acting in a charitable role they had not anticipated. On the other they were being accused by James Boyd of not living up to their responsibilities. As far as they were concerned, they had agreed to receive 100 men capable of working on the railway construction. They could not believe that Fitzwilliam had sent out entire families. Fitzwilliam's answer to their complaints was that to the Irish mind emigration was bad enough but separation from family was unthinkable. The only way to get 100 men to work on the railway in New Brunswick was to send their families with them. The railroad men were unconvinced, but nonetheless decided to uphold their part of the agreement, that is, to employ one hundred men for three months. This would give the emigrants a chance to settle in before the onslaught of their first Canadian winter.

Even this presented the company with a problem. According to a report made to the Lieutenant Governor's Office:

> Of those taken into the service of the company, some were aged and so infirm as to be almost past labour; one or two (were) over 70 years of age and one nearly blind; all enfeebled by the passage and sickness; not over one-half could be rated as able-bodied men.[20]

The heavy strain was taking its toll on Boyd and towards the end of June he could no longer carry out his duties to his own satisfaction. His son stepped into the breach, assessing the state of the immigrants both healthy and sick and 'ferreting out cases of impoverishment'.[21]

Boyd took several weeks to recuperate and by the time he felt fit enough to return the worst was over. Over the next five weeks there was a rapid decrease in the number of patients, bringing the total down to 28 in all, fourteen on the island and fourteen at the railway station. Visits to the island were reduced to three times a week as the urgency eased. Boyd reported that, in total, there had been 32 deaths. This, he said, was a small number compared with so much sickness out of the 374 persons landed on the island.[22] Among the dead were some of his hired attendants. Benjamin Tufts was one of these employees. He had been hired to erect and maintain some of the buildings on the island. A brave and compassionate man, he could not restrict his work to maintenance duties and did what he could to ease the plight of the sick. He caught the fever and died, leaving his 34-year-old wife Margaret to raise three children (two of their own and a step-daughter). Mrs Tufts was to share the destitution of the widows whose husbands had died on the *Star* or in hospital. She and her children had to seek public charity and she left the area before 1861.[23] While such stories commemorate the unselfish courage of men like Tufts they also help to explain why local inhabitants were reluctant to have anything to do with the immigrants.

In the meantime, some of the healthy *Star* passengers were already taking steps to make St Andrews their permanent home, unlike most Irish immigrants who had merely used it as a port of entry. William Mahood, the Deputy Surveyor of Charlotte County, accompanied some of Fitzwilliam's tenants to a tract of land adjacent to the railway line on which they hoped to establish a settlement. Mahood agreed that the land was suitable for such a purpose but nothing could be done until the exact location of the rail track was determined as the company had been granted a twenty-foot margin of land on either side of it.[24] While this was a valid point, it should be noted that the company had also been granted 20,000 unspecified acres with frontage along the line. This was to entice immigrants to settle along the route of the railroad but Fitzwilliam's former tenants were not offered any of this tract. They were not the 'sort of people' the company had in mind. This is evident from a letter written by John Wilson, the prime mover behind the railroad, to one of St Andrews' leading citizens.[25]

Boyd visited the provincial capital, Fredericton, in early August and on his return to St Andrews he took the last twelve people off the island and made arrangements to lock up the hospital. Among these twelve was the Jones family. Boyd believed that the family would not be able to sustain themselves for some time to come. To the others, he dispensed a small amount of money and brought the affairs of the island to a close. The deserted hospital was then scrubbed and whitewashed. There were, however, still eleven cases of sickness at O'Neill's farm on the mainland. This had been the site of the makeshift halfway house near the railway work station. All these cases were well on the way to recovery.

A less conscientious man would have then considered his duty carried out to the full but Boyd had still a great deal of work to do trying to keep the widows and orphans out of the Poor House. This can be seen from a report he sent on 12 September:

> Herewith I have ... much pleasure in announcing for His Excellency's information that the second Hospital at O'Neills farm is now closed, having got rid of all the inmates yesterday. I have still under my charge Widows and Orphans, 33 in number, at an expense of two shillings and sixpence per week each besides the house rent which is trifling.

I endeavoured to get the Commissioners of the Poor to take them into their charge and have notified them that I shall send them all to the Poor House next week. They complain that they have not the means of supporting them, even though an assessment should be ordered at the September Sessions. The difficulty of collecting it at a period of such great depression is so apparent that I don't think myself it could be collected. Our Tradesmen and Labourers have little or nothing to do at present, therefore money could not be got from them.

In the event of their going to the Poor House, the expense would be double what I am now allowing them.

You will perceive by my accounts that I am considerably in advance, and I have to request that a Warrant may issue for the Balance due me. If it is considered that my mode of providing for these people is more economical than sending them to the Poor House, I request that a further sum may be advanced to me for that purpose, as I am confidant we shall have the greater part of them to maintain through the winter.

I could, if allowed, get rid of some of the families that were bound for Canada West, by paying a part of the expense of forwarding them, in which I think there would be a great saving.[26]

When news of the plight of the passengers of the *Star* reached Fitzwilliam, Robert Challoner wrote to William Graves stating that he believed that the surgeon on board the vessel had left his duties unattended to and demanded that an enquiry be held into it.[27] Whatever explanation was given brought the matter to a close because a month later, on 26 August, Challoner again wrote to Graves expressing Fitzwilliam's satisfaction.[28]

In September, Fitzwilliam, on one of his visits to Coolattin, wrote to John Wilson inviting him to visit Wentworth House, Fitzwilliam's main home in England. Wilson agreed and duly called on Fitzwilliam at the end of that month. It was part of an extended trip to pursue political and financial support for the railway project. Wilson spent a day there, going over the plans with Fitzwilliam and his family. The earl and his eldest son, Lord Milton, seemed totally captivated by the plans. All aspects, commercial and engineering, intrigued them. Fitzwilliam's doubts about the project, if he ever had any, seemed dispelled and he urged Wilson to canvas influential people in government and business circles to become share-holders. He also told him to circulate the company prospectus and details of the company's plan to encourage more landlords to send out emigrants. To help pave the way, Fitzwilliam drew up a list of over 100 noblemen and peers whom he felt should be contacted and he allowed Wilson to use his name in support. Not surprisingly, Wilson was overjoyed by this reception and later wrote: 'The Earl and family are praised greatly by all but not half enough is said of them.'[29]

The crisis for his erstwhile tenants not only continued but deteriorated throughout the winter of 1848–9. On 2 January, the railway company wrote the following letter to James Boyd:

> The President, Directors and Company of the Saint Andrews And Quebec Rail Road Company, having employed the Emigrants sent out by Earl Fitzwilliam, Three months over and above the time agreed upon by the Company and owing to the inclemency of the weather and unproductiveness of their work at this Season, the Company cannot think of maintaining them any longer. Therefore (we) beg leave to inform you, as Emigrant Officer, that they will become a charge upon the Province, they being utterly unable to support or maintain them(selves). An answer is requested so as to know you will please take charge of them.[30]

A copy of this letter was also sent to Boyd's superiors at the Provincial Secretary's Office. This latest move incensed Boyd who had always felt that the company had treated the immigrants very badly. He sent a stinging reply to John Richard Partelow, who had replaced John Saunders as Provincial Secretary:

I regret to find that they have not stated (the) facts in relation to these people, their engagements, etc, and however disagreeable it may be for me to state the facts as they really are, I feel bound as a public officer in the conscientious discharge of my duty, to place the matter on its proper footing. First, that these people were not sent out by Earl Fitzwilliam without first making arrangements for their reception; Second, that negotiation was entered into for that purpose as early as last February with a promise on the part of the company to have places in readiness to receive them as soon as they were notified of his Lordship's intention of sending them and of which he gave the company the correct(?) notice and, though frequently urged to prepare shanties along the line of the contemplated road or other places to secure them in, nothing was done until after the vessel arrived and the passengers landed at the Quarantine Station.[31]

He went on to state that this lack of preparation consigned the emigrants to disgraceful conditions. Summarising the events of the preceding six months, he recalled how the hospital and other buildings had been grossly overcrowded, sheltering nearly 400 people. He reminded them how he had found it necessary to hire a small house and barn for the purpose of housing those that were free from sickness. Although this helped to a small degree, the new premises could not accommodate more than one-third of their number. They had been without provisions and, according to Boyd, received none from the railway company.

Those employed by the railroad found that dealing with the management was not easy. Again according to Boyd, the company had agreed with Fitzwilliam that the men would be employed for three months at two shillings and some (illegible in the original letter) pence per day. The company now said that they told the emigrants at the time of employing them that they should go to the United States when the three months were over, but Boyd stated that:

As to the company urging these people to go to the United States when their time of hiring had expired, I have reason to know to the contrary. They were told at the time that they were at liberty to go or remain where they were at the same rate of wages with an assurance that they would be employed during the winter. Subsequently, some difficulty occurred among them and the men left work. They were again employed with an understanding that if they again became refractory they would be discharged altogether since which they have conducted themselves in a becoming manner ... While writing, I am at this moment surrounded by the whole tribe of the railroad men who claim that this morning they are put on short time and this coupled with the inclemency of the weather will not allow them to work much more than three and a half days in the week. These people are really in a most deplorable situation scarcely half clad and many of them with six to ten children and all they could earn if employed full time, deducting ... for bad weather, is scarcely sufficient to provide them with the correct description of food to say nothing of shoes or other clothing. There are but four shanties built for them to live in, consequently a good number are living in hired rooms, the rent of which they will be unable to pay.

Such is the depressed state of business that the Commissioners of the Poor have neither money nor credit nor can they raise any on the amount authorised to be borrowed by them ... for the relief of ... the poor, the number of which now receiving relief is unprecedented and should this state of things continue the number will be doubled. There is not a day's work of any kind to be had nor is there a prospect of any.[32]

It will be remembered that this last remark is an echo of the reports submitted to the Poor Law Commissioners by the various Relief Committees on the Fitzwilliam estate two years previously. Crossing the Atlantic, it would seem, did little to change the fortunes of the emigrants. Another interesting aspect of this letter was Boyd's reference to the company's claim that the Irish workers had 'become refractory'. Perhaps their attitude to the company had hardened when they realised that indigenous labourers working with the surveying crews were receiving five shillings a day, more than double what the immigrants were paid.[33]

Boyd urged the Province to intervene because if something was not done to relieve the situation the emigrants would, in all probability, resort to crime to maintain themselves. He asked for £150 which 'if judicially applied amongst the largest families I think would do much in carrying them to (when) spring opens, this sum to be independent of the amount required for the support of the 40 and more widows and children already in my hands. It will be found more economical and a greater saving to the province than to place them in the charge of the Commissioners of the Poor'.[34]

These statements by Boyd had the effect of mobilising the Lieutenant Governor's Office and Asa Coy was sent to St Andrews to look into the matter. He arrived in the town on 22 January and spent the following day meeting James Boyd, representatives of the railroad company and Robert Kee, a Commissioner of the Poor. It soon became obvious that the destitution which had been complained of was confined to the immigrants who had arrived eight months earlier in early summer. Accompanied by Boyd, Coy visited eight of the poorest families, totalling 45 people. The following is taken from his report to the Lieutenant Governor:

Widow Terney has four children and an orphan. This woman's husband died on the passage.
Widow Birne has six children; one boy at work on the railway at 1s.3d. per day. This woman's husband died on the passage.
Mary Kelly has no husband. She is sick in bed, has an infant and young sister to provide for.
Widow Furlong has six children, all young girls. Her husband

died at the Quarantine Station.

Widow Kerron has two children. Her husband died at the time of embarkation.

Widow Neil has two children. Her husband died on the passage. She is partly supported by the labour of one son on the Rail Road.

Widow Byrne has eight children. Her husband died on the passage. She has two sons at work on the Rail Road

All these parties are very destitute of clothing, especially the children.

Coy also visited families who were in rented rooms and shanties:

1. IN HIRED ROOMS:

Edward Carr was at work. He has a widowed sister resident with him and occupies a room near the town.

Thomas Kearon was also at work. He has a wife and six children and occupies a room near Carr's.

John Summers was also at work. He has a wife and six children and occupies a room near Carr's.

John Poppin (i.e. Popham) has a sick wife, an infant at the breast, and two small children. This man works when the state of his family permits his leaving them. The family is very destitute, half-naked, very filthy, and apparently in a starving condition. Mr Whitlock (the railway company secretary) represents Poppin as very industrious, sober, quiet, and very kind and attentive to his wife and children.

There are some other families also occupying hired rooms whom I was prevented from seeing. Mr Whitlock furnished me with the following memorandum of such cases: –

Patrick Knowlin (i.e. Nowlan or Nolan) has a wife and five children. Himself and some of the children are sickly.

Robert Heras (*sic* – this is a mistranscription of Hues/Hughes) has a wife and five children destitute of clothing. The woman has been sick all summer and still continues so, and the man loses part of his working time attending to her.

2. IN SHANTIES ERECTED BY THE RAIL ROAD COMPANY

In No. 1. Five families, 25 persons, men, women and children. The father of one family, Lawrence Neil, is lame and unable to work. He has a wife and one child. They have subsisted by charity for some time.

In No. 2. Four families, sixteen souls, men, women and children. One couple has eight small children. John Doyt (*sic* – probably Doyle), without wife or child, is lame and at present unable to work.

In No. 3. Two families, ten souls in all. These are more comfortable, being less crowded than in Nos. 1 and 2.

In No. 4. Four families, sixteen souls; one is an orphan child; three are cripples:

John Burns and his wife are aged and infirm, the man 67, his wife 75 years of age, both now nearly past labour. The man works occasionally, and I afterwards found him with the gang at work, receiving full wages, 2s.6d. per day.

John Cole (i.e. Call) is lame and unable to work. He has a wife and four children and has been allowed support by the company.

Mary Burn and her husband have three small children. The man is able to work, the woman is near her confinement, and very poorly destitute of wearing apparel and bed clothes. She complains of unkind treatment from the other females, some of whom are her relations and live in the same shanty.

In No.5. One family, seven children, nine souls. Mother well, father sick and at present unable to earn anything; a child sick also.

3. AT WORK IN GANGS

I found 79 men and boys. They are all poorly clothed for this inclement season of the year, and more especially so for outdoor work. Some of the men are aged and infirm, one nearly blind, another partially disabled by frost bites.

In my interview with the Railway Company Directors, the responsibility of the company with respect to these emigrants was discussed, and their intentions stated. Lord Fitzwilliam, by whom these emigrants were sent out, appears to have acted in good faith; and the correspondence which was submitted to me, showed that the company had been careful not to hold out better prospects than the nature of the case would seem to warrant.

While the company, in consenting to receive 100 men, under a pledge of the means of affording employment to them for three months, at the rate of two shillings sterling per day, might naturally expect 100 men without the encumbrance of families. His Lordship, on the other hand, might have felt justified in sending out, with the able-bodied, such a number of aged, infirm, and young, as would not in Ireland or Great Britain be considered an excessive burden.

Of the number shipped, it was stated that 374 souls were landed on the Quarantine Island, a large portion of whom were ill with fever, either at the time of leaving the vessel, or whilst they remained at Quarantine, and a number died. Of those taken into the service of the company, some were aged and so infirm as to be almost past labour; one or two over 70 years of age, and one nearly blind; all enfeebled by the passage and sickness; not over one half could be rated as able-bodied men. They were all poorly clothed and destitute of bedding. The term during which his Lordship expected them to be employed expired on the last day of September, up to which period, such as had been employed by the company, were paid 2s.6d. currency per day. Foreseeing in some measure the difficulty of Winter maintenance, and as they were not found to be profitable labourers, the company then discharged them, and advised them to make their way to the United States. A few left, but soon returned, and the whole were again set to work at the same rate of wages for working time.

The President (of the railway company) further stated that the company had exhausted their available means; that they had incurred much unanticipated expense on account of these people as well before they went to work as afterwards, and under these circumstances the company intended to employ them no longer than the 1st of next April.

This intention, however, was rescinded at a meeting of the

company held on the 26th and their resolution not to employ any of the parties after the then next week was communicated to me by letter from the President received while on my journey to Fredericton.[35]

Coy went on to describe the critical financial position in St Andrews. Demand on the town coffers far exceeded supply. Parish annual income comprised rent receipts on about 1,000 acres of cultivated land amounting to £141 ('not very punctually paid'), £4 from a tax on dogs; and about £10 from fines for breaches of the Acts of Assembly – making a total of £155 a year. Another £100 was raised from Poor Rates, making a grand total of £255. The influx of destitute emigrants and the needs of indigenous paupers needed greater funds than these. Many of the local poor were out of work owing to both a rope factory and a ship under construction being destroyed by fire the previous year. These factors contributed to the stagnation of the local economy and the inability of the town to assist the ever-increasing pauper population. A list of people in receipt of assistance was attached to the report, all the names are familiar from Fitzwilliam's Emigration Book.

On 26 January, Coy was handed a letter by John Wilson, expressing the company's delight in laying what they believed to be the true facts of the matter before him:

I am very much pleased and relieved by the course His Excellency has adopted in this matter as I have every reason to suppose the Governor has been misinformed on the Situation of these people.

We are now in the most unpleasant dilemma with these people, as it was our intention to have kept them at work till Spring, but owing to the awful state of the Country, and our not being able to collect from Stockholders one penny, and all our Railway funds being exhausted, the Board have this day determined to discontinue employing them after next week, and what will become of them I am greatly perplexed to know.

You will notice by the several letters from Earl Fitzwilliam that 100 ABLE BODIED MEN were all we had any reason to expect but, to our surprise, with the 100 men sent out were 277 old men, women, and children, and the whole afflicted with sickness, death, and poverty.

I am sure that you will see that we have employed those men and boys principally out of charity, as their work is not worth sixpence per day, being so enfeebled by the voyage and sickness, that but few of the men were able to do a day's work.

Already many of the poor have suffered much, and unless aid is obtained from some quarter, their state will be desperate.

We asked the Government last Fall for assistance to settle these people on Crown Land at the head of the Digdeguash River and to be repaid by them in the same manner as the Harvey Settlers have done. If this had been complied with very much toil and expense would have been avoided.[36]

The reference to settling the immigrants on Crown Land made it clear, if clarification were needed, that the railway company had no intention of allowing them to settle on any of the 20,000 acres it had been allocated.

While all this was going on, Boyd was mindful that within a few short months, spring would arrive and with it more ships of destitute people. Five of the buildings on Hospital Island were dilapidated. He requested £160 to do whatever was necessary to make them ready for the new arrivals.[37] The following month, February, he acknowledged the receipt of 40 overcoats and 100 pairs of shoes for the use of the emigrants of the *Star*.

By this time, the emigrants were tired of living off charity. They had left Ireland in the hope of making something of their lives. They wanted to put down roots in St Andrews and show that, given the opportunity, they would prove to be decent, respectable members of the community. But how were they to achieve this? Their request for land, which they were willing to pay for if given the opportunity, back in July had been refused. In March, with the support of some of the town's leading citizens, they wrote to the Lieutenant Governor, Edmund Wicker.[38]

To His Excellency, Sir Edmund Wicker, Head Lieutenant Governor and Commander-in-Chief in and for the Province of New Brunswick; the Honourable the Legislative Council; and the Honourable the Assembly of New Brunswick.

The Memorial of the Undersigned residents of the parish of Saint Andrews in the County of Charlotte,

Most Humbly Sheweth

That the memorialists and their families, now numbering about 280 individuals, arrived in Saint Andrews aforesaid in the ship *Star* from Ireland in the month of May last, having prior to their leaving Ireland engaged with the Agent of the Earl Fitzwilliam to work on the Saint Andrews and Quebec Railroad for a limited period.

That for the last three months your memorialists have only been partially employed on the said line of Railroad in consequence of which your memorialists have not been able to earn enough to enable them to provide their families with a sufficiency of the most coarse food. Your memorialists being discharged from all further labour on the said Road (owing, as they understand, to the want of means to prosecute the undertaking) leaving your memorialists wholly destitute.

Your memorialists would most respectfully observe that they have always been and now are desirous to settle in the Province, they would fain hope that their conduct since their arrival had been such as to gain the approbation of those who know them and be a guarantee for their future good behaviour.

Owing to your memorialists extreme poverty, they are unable to locate themselves in the Public Domain, they therefore pray your Excellency and Honours to grant to each of their families a location ticket for 50 acres of land, somewhere on the Woodstock and Oakby road, the place to be hereafter selected, and to advance them such sums of money from time to time as will enable them to subsist for one year, for which lands and advances your memorialists are willing to pay by instalments.

And should your Excellency and Honours not comply with your memorialists request in this instance, they would further pray that your Excellency and Honours would make them a grant of such a sum of money as would enable your memorialists to remove with their families to Canada West or make such order in that premises as to your Excellency and Honours may soon meet

And your memorialists as in duty bound will ever pray.

Saint Andrews, March 31st, 1849

John Bulger, David Kerwan, Francis McDonald, John Burn, Denis O'Neill, Thomas Lawler, William Farrell, James Githings, Laurence O'Neill, Michael Caffrey, John Byrne, John Doyle, Peter Carroll, Michael Keely, Patrick Tyrrell, Patrick ???, John Doyle, John Kavanagh, Michael Walsh, John Call, Morgan Walsh, Edward Carr, Patrick Kirwan, Batt Toole, John Summers, William Moles, John Burns, John McCann, James Burns, John Casey, Robert Hues, Andrew O'Neill, John Burns, William ???, John Mooney, John Burns, Patrick Waydick, Simon Burns, Patrick Doyle, James Burns, Patrick Burns, Joseph Burns, Thomas Beane, John Owens, John Green, John Kelley, John Burns, John Doyle, Robert White, Daniel Downs, John Popham, John Dempsey, Michael Cummins, John Conron, Simon Burns, Patrick Priestley, John Hyland, James O'Neill, Patrick Nowlan, Thomas Maher, Thomas Mulhall, John Ballans.

This was undersigned by several respected members of the community, including John Wilson. Their altruism was probably more than a little tinged with the desire to simply get the memorialists off their hands. As in the previous July, this request was refused.

Things should have been improving by the end of March, but they were not. On 30 March, all the *Star* emigrants who were working on the railroad were discharged by the company.

They were destitute and Boyd attributed that destitution to 'small wages and short time'. They immediately applied to him for assistance and he wrote to the Lieutenant Governor's Office to see if he was authorised to help. Four days later, the magistrates of St Andrews also wrote to the Lieutenant Governor's Office stating that the destitute emigrants were now roaming the streets in a half-starved condition and threatening that if they did not get assistance they would take what they needed. The inhabitants of the town begged the Lieutenant Governor to meet the needs of these people until they could be 'got rid of' as the local coffers were exhausted.[39]

By April, many of the emigrants were dependent on the meat and molasses provided by the Province and Boyd could see no end to their plight. With the influx of the new emigrants imminent, he asked for money to assist those already in St Andrews to leave the area, rather than to feed them. He suggested that £150 would get many of them on their way to Boston, Portland or Bangor, whichever took the least money. It is interesting to note that all three proposed destinations were in the United States and not Canada. There were several valid reasons for wanting the emigrants to move on from St Andrews. Local business was at a standstill and the indigenous population were finding it difficult enough to get work for themselves. In such circumstances, it was unreasonable to expect them to feed and shelter a constant stream of newly-arrived destitute people in their small town. Money was scarce and goodwill scarcer. Even if the townspeople had been financially capable of feeding so many refugees, and even if their goodwill was inexhaustible, the imminent arrival of more ship-loads of immigrants made it logistically impracticable. It was a question of making room and the only way to do that was to push last year's emigrants onwards. Once the offer of free or assisted passage into the United States was made, it would be up to the immigrants themselves to go or stay but if they opted to stay they would have to fend for themselves and would be no longer entitled to relief. It was a repeat of what they had faced a year earlier in Ireland. Then they had been urged to emigrate to Canada or starve in Ireland whilst now it was move on to the United States or starve in New Brunswick.[40]

Despite these urgings a surprising number of *Star* passengers remained in the St Andrews area. According to the 1851 Census, over 60% of them were still there three years after their arrival. Many of these lived in the Waweig district which was adjacent to the railway line, opposite Hospital Island. This was where the shanties had been erected and by the time the census was taken 40% of the houses there were still described as such, or as cabins or log houses. In 1861, 25% of the passengers of the *Star* were still in St Andrews. Several families were to live the rest of their lives there. Robert Hughes, for example, died in his St Andrews home in 1894. His wife, Margaret, survived him by a year dying at the age of 86. Michael Caffrey was also a resident of St Andrews until his death in 1885. His wife Mary died nine years later. Intermarriage between the *Star* families also took place. Michael Cummings married Ellen Furlong's daughter Ann, and William Leonard married Catherine Hyland. There is no record of the fate of the White children who lost their father at sea and their mother two days after arrival. Perhaps they were put in an orphanage or adopted by a local family. It is also likely they were adopted by fellow passengers and moved west.

It has been possible to trace the fortunes of one extended family who had arrived on the *Star*. Thomas Mulhall lived in the townland of Lascoleman (now Liscolman) on the western edge of the estate. He was 49 when the clearance policy was implemented and his name, with those of his family, was entered in the Emigration Book in 1847. His wife, Bridget, was a daughter of the neighbouring Kealy (or Kealey/Keeley) family and her parents and siblings were also registered to emigrate that year. For some reason their departure was delayed for twelve months but when the 1848 exodus got under way, the Kealy and Mulhall families made their way to New Ross and boarded the *Star*.

The patriarch was 60-year-old Daniel Kealy. One record puts his age at 70 but this is incorrect. With him were his wife Catherine (54), son Michael (33), daughter Mary (23), son John (21), and daughter Catherine (17). His eldest daughter Anne had been listed to go in 1847 but her name did not appear on the passenger list the following year. She might have died in the intervening year and this might have been the reason for the delay. Daniel's other daughter, Bridget Mulhall (37), and her family, husband Thomas, Catherine (7), Mary (5), Ann (3), and infant Thomas, completed the group. According to the 1851 New Brunswick Census, baby Thomas was born in New Brunswick, but an infant Thomas is on the passenger list in 1848 so must have been born in Ireland. Perhaps the Irish-born Thomas died and his mother may have followed the custom of the time by naming a newly-born son in Canada Thomas in memory of his dead brother. Also, according to the 1847 Emigration Book, the Mulhalls had another daughter, Mary, who was three years old at that time. Her name did not appear on the passenger list the following year.

None of the Kealys or Mulhalls died during the voyage but the horrors of shipboard life had taken their toll on 60-year-old Daniel and he died at St Andrews on 7 June, just ten days after the ship's arrival. The able-bodied of the family went to work on the railway. According to the 1851 Census, Michael Keeley (as the name was spelled in this record) and John were both railroad labourers, as was Thomas Mulhall. Both families were living in shanties.

As we have seen, life was far from pleasant but the will to survive overrode all other factors and the Keeleys and Mulhalls made the best of their situation. The Mulhalls added to their family and moved across the river to Pembroke, Maine. Pembroke was a booming coastal town in the mid-1800s, due to shipping and iron works but according to the 1860 Census, Thomas was employed as a farm labourer. The eldest child, Catherine, was now seventeen and working as a servant girl, and, presumably, her contribution to the family coffers also improved their lives. Their last child, Maria, whom the family called Nellie, was born in 1863. By 1870, Thomas owned four acres of improved land, worth about $200. He also had two milk cows, one other 'piece of cattle', and four swine. Five years later, Bridget is recorded as buying another eighteen acres for $144.

When Thomas died in 1887, he was concerned for the welfare of Nellie who did not enjoy good health. To protect her interests, he willed the farmstead to her but with the proviso that Daniel should live there and work the farm for the benefit of both. If Daniel provided for his sister for the duration of her life, the farm would become his on her demise. It seemed a reasonable arrangement but Nellie's health deteriorated and her medical expenses increased so the farm had to be sold. However, Daniel did manage to buy back a small portion at a later time.

The year of Nellie's birth, 1863, Catherine was twenty years old and she married a mariner, James Aylward. James was lost at sea some time in the 1870s, leaving Catherine with seven children to support. She moved to the larger town of Calais, not far from Pembroke, where she lived out the remainder of her life with one of her daughters and, later, with a grandson. She died in 1929 at the age of 87. Despite her courage and strength of character, she was never to break loose from poverty. As was so often the case with Irish immigrants fleeing famine, it was to take several generations to break through the economic and social barriers. Their struggle against circumstance and prejudice instilled in their descendants a strength that can only come from adversity.[41]

The McDaniel family lost more than most in their transition from Ireland to Canada. They not only lost several members of the family who died en route or soon after arrival but they also lost their name, becoming McDonald in all lists in which they were registered. In most official documents, people were asked their names by public employees unused to Irish accents. These enumerators wrote what they thought they heard. In this way, several Byrne families became Burn or Burns, Call was transcribed as Cole and sometimes Caul, Giddens (or Gethings) became Gideon, and Popham became Poppin. Despite the changed spellings, many of these families can be traced in the records as being long-term residents of St Andrews. In the words of Gail Campbell and Ruth Bleasdale: 'Although St Andrews, the only port of entry in Charlotte County, received shiploads of immigrants fleeing famine in Ireland in 1847 and 1849 as well as 1848, the majority of those landing had no intention of staying, even for a brief period ... Only the passengers of the *Star* would have a significant impact on the Parish of St Andrews'.[42]

The railway project was a failure. The start-stop nature of the enterprise saw only nine miles of track completed in four years. Across the river, in the US, a rival company completed a line connecting Portland with Quebec in the same period. John Wilson, whose dream had disintegrated, lost much of his fortune and died in 1856. The route was eventually completed by a new company. That Fitzwilliam's belief (and financial interest) in this project had not waned is reflected in the fact that in June 1852 his niece, Mrs Murray, turned the first sod on the next stage of the route[43] and that one of the locomotives built for the company in 1857 was named *Earl Fitzwilliam*.[44]

AT THE ESTATE

While all this was going on in New Brunswick throughout the winter of 1848/9, plans for the 1849 phase of the clearance programme were well under way. The local newspaper, the *Wexford Independent*, (there was no newspaper published in County Wicklow at that time) carried advertisements of regular sailings to Liverpool from where emigrants could travel across the Atlantic. They could also sail directly to Atlanta, New York and Baltimore from the ports of Wexford and New Ross. Reports of mass emigration from neighbouring counties were also featured. In March, William Graves advertised that the *Jane* and *Aberfoyle* would sail for Quebec the following month. These were the vessels on which the next batch of Fitzwilliam tenants would sail. Robert Challoner had identified the families he intended to emigrate that year. In some cases he added more information beside their names in the Emigration Book, such as the name of the ship on which they were to travel and the words 'Chest' and 'Graves'. This indicated that the family would be taking a luggage chest with them and that William Graves would be informed of the relevant details about each particular family.[45] Ninety-six families, comprising 632 people, were entered in the emigration list that year.

Chapter 9

1850–6

1850

The spring of 1850 opened with a flurry of advertisements in the local press regarding emigration. Prospective emigrants could take a ship to New South Wales or California, New York or Georgia. William Graves still concentrated on the Canadian trade. In March he advertised that the *Aberfoyle* and the *India* would sail from New Ross for Quebec on 1 April and 20 April respectively. The *Juno* and the *Triton* followed in May and June. As a footnote, he added: 'Owing to the small number of persons who landed at Quebec last year, it is expected that tradesmen, labourers, etc, landing there this Spring will find good demand for their services and those bound for the western portions of the United States or Canada will find Quebec the cheapest landing port, from the great extent of cheap inland water up the St Lawrence and the lakes of America.' This cheery note was used throughout the season and was more a marketing strategy than a statement of fact.

At the same time, another 44 families, 346 people, had been earmarked for emigration from the Fitzwilliam estate and these were allocated spaces on those ships. On 15 June, the *Wexford Independent* reported:

> We are glad to learn that the ships *India* and *Aberfoyle*, the property of Messrs Graves of Ross, arrived safely in Quebec after

quick passages and landed their passengers, numbering about 700, in good health.

Four days later it went much further:

It affords us much pleasure to insert the following letter, which has been received from one of the emigrants of the ship *India* which was dispatched by Messrs Graves & Son, New Ross, this season ...

Quebec 14 May 1850

Dear Mr —

As I promised to write to you on my arriving here, I now hasten to fulfil that promise. We came to anchor on 11th May after experiencing some heavy weather; and, at one time, I thought we were in danger, on account of meeting a great deal of ice; but owing to the watchful eye and experience of Captain Williams, and an expert crew, the ship was got about before we touched it. My tongue cannot express to you the merit that is due to Captain Williams, for the manner in which he acted towards all the passengers, and his anxiety to make us comfortable and preserve our health by cleansing, fumigating, etc, and I am thankful to say that the best results followed his labours, for no symptoms of sickness appeared. We had six deaths on board, three were infants born on the passage, and three were very old people who were nearly dead before they left Ireland.

Before leaving the ship, the passengers returned their warm and sincere thanks to Captain Willis,[1] Captain Williams, the Doctor and crew for their uniform kindness; and with repeated prayers for their prosperity, we took our leave of the *India*.

John Hanlon

(Editor's note —The ice referred to in the letter sank 14 vessels with up to 500 lives lost. One of these was an emigrant ship from Derry with 80–100 passengers all of whom were lost. April and May are bad months for ice-floes with breaking-up of frost in the Arctic seas. This year worst for many years.)

The Ships:

India – Advertised in the *Wexford Independent* as 'new, 1,400 tons Capt Williams, 9 feet between decks'. Left New Ross on 9 April and arrived in Quebec on 19 May, a passage of 40 days. She had 411 passengers on board.

Aberfoyle – Advertised in the *Wexford Independent* as 900 tons. According to Lloyd's register she was a 496 ton barque, built in Nova Scotia in 1845. Her A1 classification had expired by 1850. She left on 25 April and completed the voyage, date not known with 280 passengers.

Juno – Advertised in the *Wexford Independent* as 'Beautiful and very fast sailing ship 1,260 tons, 9 feet between decks, Capt J Moran'. According to Waterford harbour records she was 783 tons.[2] Left on 24 May with a cargo of salt, four cabin passengers and 381 people travelling steerage. They arrived at Grosse Île in the last days of June with 374 passengers.

Triton – Advertised in the *Wexford Independent* as 1,300 tons, Captain J. Smith. According to Lloyd's Register she was 676 tons, ship-rig, built in Nova Scotia in 1839. Her A1 classification had expired in 1850. Sailed from New Ross on 13 June and arrived at Quebec 42 days later on 25 July with a cargo of salt and 371 passengers.[3]

1851

In the spring of 1851 another 81 families, comprising 483 individuals, emigrated from the Coolattin estate. Many of these were scheduled to sail to Quebec. The *Wexford Independent* advertised that the ship *India* would leave New Ross for Quebec on 1 April. She was, according to the advertisement inserted by Graves, of 1,400 tons burden, a fine vessel for the time. The same advertisement announced the scheduled sailing of the *Glenlyon* two weeks later on 15 April, also for Quebec. The *Glenlyon* was described as 'a remarkable fine and fast ship' of 1,700 tons. On 21 June, the newspaper reported: 'We are happy to state that the fine ships *India* and *Glenlyon* which sailed from the port of Ross to Quebec having upwards of 900 passengers on board all safely landed.'

There had long been the belief that sailing directly from an Irish port to the United States or Canada was somehow the last resort of those who simply could not afford to go through Liverpool. While it was generally conceded that the American-owned vessels which operated out of that port were better manned and equipped, there were also major drawbacks to it which did not exist in the smaller Irish ports such as New Ross.

On 15 March, the editor of the *Wexford Independent* printed a warning that had previously appeared in a Kilkenny paper:

Caution to Emigrants:
Several cases of the most shocking fraud practised recently upon our poor people emigrating from this county have come within our knowledge, we deem it only proper in compassion for this class of persons to give some advice which may lead those intending to leave this district for America during the present Spring in the right course. The Liverpool low-ship agents have 'crimps' employed throughout Ireland to entrap passengers; and the unwary who enter their toils find, too late, the loss of time and money, and the increased length of passage to which they are subjected by embarking at Liverpool, in place of selecting some of their neighbouring Irish ports. For the people of our country, who are resolved upon making their fortune in the 'New World', no port affords the convenience which New Ross, the nearest station for emigrant vessels, supplies and we would recommend them by all means to give it preference over Liverpool.

The sufferings experienced by the emigrants leaving by the port of Liverpool during the past winter have scarcely ever been paralleled. Many of the American emigrant vessels had to return after 70 to 100 days suffering on the Atlantic and, of course, with all the stores laid in for the voyage by the deluded passengers exhausted. Ships from the harbour of Ross[4] are at sea at once, whilst from Liverpool they have a long, tedious and dangerous coasting voyage to endure.

We give this advice purely to benefit the poor people intending to emigrate and with the hope of saving them much needless hardship and loss of means. We have no interest whatever in the success of any parties connected with either of the ports referred to.

This was not scaremongering. Agitation to have something done about the chaotic situation in Liverpool had been under way for some time, with even the Conservative newspapers lending support to the proposal to have a government-run depot for transient emigrants.

THE SHIPS

India – which had also been used in 1850, sailed on 6 April with 430 passengers. She reached Quebec on 11 May after 35 days.

Glenlyon – Advertised in *Wexford Independent* as 'remarkably fine and fast, 1,700 tons'. According to Lloyd's register she was 908 tons. She had been built in New Brunswick in 1841. She sailed on 22 April and arrived 37 days later on 29 May with 478 passengers.

Pilgrim – Advertised in the *Wexford Independent* as 'a new ship, 1700 tons, Captain Jones'. Lloyd's Register agreed she was new, built in Quebec in 1850 but with a tonnage of 824. Her classification with Lloyd's was A1. She sailed on 10 May and arrived at Quebec on 14 June, a passage of 35 days. She carried 485 passengers.[5]

1852

In 1852 the clearances continued with 330 individuals, comprising 53 families, leaving their homes.

In several instances, the amount of 'support', as in 'passage

& support', was entered in the side notes. For example, Matt McDaniel and his family from Sleaghcoyle received ten shillings per head in addition to free passage. Andy Loughlin of Mullins received fifteen shillings each for himself, his wife and their nine-year-old daughter Jane. Their fifteen-year-old son James was scratched from the list without any reason given.

THE SHIPS

Confiance, according to Lloyd's Register, was 824 tons and had been built in Quebec in 1851. Interestingly, she was listed as being engaged in the Australia trade. She was classified A1. She left New Ross on 1 May with a cargo of salt and 482 passengers. She had a slow voyage and arrived in Quebec 48 days later on 17 June.

Lord Ashburton – no details. She sailed on 14 May with three cabin passengers and 411 in steerage.

The 10 July issue of the *Wexford Independent* announced that both were in Quebec with the passengers in 'good health after quick and pleasant voyages'. The voyage of almost seven weeks for the *Confiance* could not, even then, have been described as 'quick', nor is it likely to have been 'pleasant' for the almost 500 steerage passengers.

1853

The first shipment of emigrants from the Fitzwilliam estate in 1853 was scheduled to sail from New Ross on board the *Dunbrody*. This plan had to be changed when the vessel could not make it on time and had to be substituted by the *Petrel*. Of the 63 families entered for emigration that spring, *Dunbrody* was written against 39 of them. Because of the substitution these could have gone out on the *Petrel* but if the *Dunbrody* was used a few weeks later they could have gone on that vessel. Many of those who emigrated in that year had only a cabin and kitchen garden whilst others had holdings varying in size from one to eighteen acres.

THE SHIPS

Dunbrody – advertised as being 850 tons but according to Lloyd's Register she was 485 tons and had been built in Quebec in 1845. She was owned by Graves & Son. Her A1 classification had expired. She was the ship used in 1847.

Petrel – was owned by Gibbs & Company of Liverpool and was a fully-rigged ship of 781 tons. She was built in St John in 1849 and had an A1 classification.

Harmony – was advertised as being a 1450 ton ship. There was no entry for her in Lloyd's Register.

Graves advertisements announced that: 'The above large and superior ships will be fitted up in the most approved manner for cabin, 2nd class and steerage passengers; these ships are well ventilated and lofty between decks, having a height of about nine feet; they are to carry experienced surgeons; and passengers by them will be supplied with water, fuel, bread stuffs, groceries, etc, according to the new government scale.'[6]

Rubbishing the opposition (often with total justification, it must be said) was another marketing tool. While Graves or the other Wexford shipbrokers do not seem to have engaged in it directly, they no doubt applauded the actions of the editor of the *Wexford Independent* when he printed the following warning to intending passengers: 'Passengers are warned against preceding to America in large three-decked ships from their over-crowded state and want of ventilation the lower or third deck which is below the water level and deficient of light, the mortality of late has in consequence been excessive. These three-decked ships sail from Liverpool and other English ports. Parties sailing from the

South of Ireland save 250 miles of their journey besides escaping the Liverpool impositions and expenses.'

1854

A total of 51 families, comprising 293 people, were entered in the Emigration Book in 1854. There were a few individuals whom the estate did not allow to go. For example, Michael Keoghoe of Tombreane numbered thirteen-year-old Betty among his children but her name was scratched from the list and the note 'no such person – not living with this man' was added. This happened with other families as well. In several such cases those not allowed were adults but what would happen to thirteen-year-old Betty? The McCann family, also at Tombreane, were in the same situation. Fifteen-year-old Winny was scratched from the list because she 'was not living with this man'. The most detailed and interesting side-note in 1854 referred to Mary Murphy of Knockloe. She was a 44-year-old widow (presumably) with four children. Betty was 21, Pat 16, Catherine 13 and Thomas 10.

> A tenant of Knockloe some time ago, now an inmate of Shillelagh Workhouse. The ratepayers in the Electoral Division agreed with Mr Challoner to pay half the expense of emigrating this family, but it is discovered now, April 18th, 1854, that the sum advanced for the purpose, £10-18-3, does not cover half the expense.

Catherine had originally been marked down as fourteen, which under the Passenger Act would make her an adult and her fare would reflect this. In the creative accountancy which took place to keep the expense of emigrating this family down to a minimum, Catherine miraculously shed a few months and her age was changed to thirteen, thereby making her a half statute adult. The cost then became:

3 adults and 2 children	= 4 statute adults
@ £4-17-6 per adult	= £18-10-0
Pension(?) & clothing	= £ 5-00-0
Pocket money	= £ 2-10-0
Total	£ 26-00-0
Lodged	£10-18-0
ditto	£ 1-04-0
	£12-02-0

(The total shown in the book was £12- 2-6, a discrepancy of 6d)
Leaving a balance to be raised of £13-17-6, actually £13-18-0.

Every now and then, Challoner, or whoever wrote the entries in the Emigration Books, would add notes which throw some light on the policies of the clearance.

Thomas Murphy, Kilmalone (ms ref 45):
Has not resided with her husband for the last two years. Supposed that William Kavanagh and son will try to get ... (illegible) ... instead'. A letter was pinned to this entry: – 'I would feel much obliged to Mr Ralph Laurenson to see that the bearer, Mary Murphy, wife of Thomas Murphy formerly of Kilmalone and now in America, be put on Lord Fitzwilliam's emigration list for the year 1854'. Signed D. Kavanagh CC, Annacurra, Jan 30th 1854.

Fr Kavanagh was the curate in charge of the church at Annacurra. His parish priest based at Killaveny (or Rockingham as it was usually referred to in the Fitzwilliam Papers) also wrote a letter that year.

Anne Lynch, Glenphillippeen (ms ref 49):
'I hereby certify that the bearer Anne Lynch of Glenphillippeen has been nursing a deserted child, called John, these four years 16th September next, whom she wishes to bring with her to America, if she were enabled to pay his passage'. Signed W. Synnott PP, Rockingham, May 10th, 1853.

THE SHIPS

Albatross – according the *Wexford Independent*, this vessel was bound for Australia. This was verified by Lloyd's Register the following year which stated that she was engaged in voyages to Melbourne. She was owned by Gibbs & Company of Liverpool and was 965 tons, built at St John with an A1 Lloyd's classification.

By the autumn of 1854, over 5,500 men, women and children had been cleared from the Fitzwilliam estate in County Wicklow. In a few isolated cases tenants earmarked for emigration refused to go but the vast majority did cross the Atlantic.

1855–6:

The clearance programme was now in its final stages and during 1855 and 1856 combined only twelve families were added to the emigration lists. Eight of these families, comprising 37 individuals, went in 1855. One family, the Doyles from Kilballyowen, refused to go to Canada. The following year, the last of this particular clearance programme, saw only four families moved off the estate.

THE SHIPS:

Woodstock – this 887 ton ship was owned by Graves & Son. She had been built in Quebec in 1850 and had an A1 classification. According to Lloyd's she was engaged in the Australia trade.

Chapter 10

CONCLUSION

By any yardstick, the clearance programme carried out on the Coolattin estate between 1847 and 1856 was a massive undertaking – and a costly one. William Graves charged the estate £3-8-6 for each tenant shipped, but this was not the total cost per head by any means. As can be seen from the general ledgers, the estate provided oatmeal and rice to supplement the emigrants' diet during the voyage. The sea chests were paid for by the estate, as was the carriage of people and luggage from the estate to New Ross. There was also the very large cost of enticing people to surrender their holdings. All in all, between 1848 and 1856, the programme cost Fitzwilliam £16,342-11-1. I have yet to find the costs incurred in 1847, but more than one-third of the entire emigrant number left the estate in that first year so the likely cost would have been about £8,000, making a grand total of approximately £24,000: a massive amount at that time, but a wise investment in the long term. The 'Surplus People' had been disposed of and the structure of the estate altered irrevocably.

The impact of the Fitzwilliam clearances during the period under review can be best assessed in relation to the population figures of the region, and can be found in the Census returns for 1841, 1851 and 1861.

It is immediately clear that the programme had a varying impact on the different townlands. When the numbers of people

127

who emigrated between 1847 and 1856 are expressed as percentages of the 1841 census figures in each townland the results range from less than 10% to over 90%. In some townlands, the clearances accounted for most of the population decline, but in other areas other factors were at work. For example, in Tomcoyle no one was listed for emigration between 1847 and 1850, yet the population fell from 74 to 27. Some unexpected trends emerge. For example, some townlands (such as Ballinavortha and Moyne) show population increases between 1841 and 1851.

It is important to consider the numbers of inmates in both the Shillelagh and Rathdrum Workhouses when looking at the population. Neither existed in 1841 yet in 1851 there were 826 people in the Shillelagh Workhouse and 1,180 in Rathdrum. By 1861 these figures had fallen to 168 and 310 respectively.

The Coolattin estate no longer exists. Towards the end of the nineteenth century, the Land League, an organisation formed to bring an end to landlordism by constitutional means, pushed through major legislative changes in the British parliament. The 1880s saw it at its most powerful, mainly because Ireland teetered on the brink of another catastrophic famine. Many of the estates of the 'landed gentry' were already bankrupt. The system which had prevailed for so long was unravelling by itself. One of the main changes was the establishment of the Land Commission. This government agency bought out encumbered properties and sold them to the people who farmed them, payments to be made on an instalments basis. For the first time, tenants could see a future in which the land they worked would be their own land, the rewards of their labour would be their own rewards and would not be handed over to an often absentee landlord. It was a social revolution.

Thus, the big estates began to shrink or disappear altogether. The Fitzwilliams sold off large sections of their, by then, 90,000 acres but they held onto Coolattin demesne for many decades. People who remember the later earls speak highly of them and their families. Their liberalism seemed undiminished as the old ways began to disappear. They finally sold Coolattin House and the surrounding acreage they had retained in the early 1970s. In 1996, Coolattin Golf Club bought the 'big house' which had for so long been the hub of this great estate, and a great deal of work has been carried out to convert it into the course clubhouse.

As part of the national Year of the Gathering, in September 2013, a two-day seminar and exhibition recalling the Famine clearances was held in Coolattin House, attended by many descendants of those who story is told within these pages.

Appendix 1

The Passengers of the *Star*

This is a record of the families who left the Fitzwilliam Estate in County Wicklow, Ireland for St Andrews, New Brunswick in Canada. They sailed on board the *Star*, leaving New Ross, County Wexford on 21 April 1848 and arriving in St Andrews on 28 May 1848. The information is taken from the Fitzwilliam Emigration Books (National Library of Ireland, MS 4974 & 4975), a list of the people scheduled to sail on the *Star* (Fitzwilliam Papers, National Library of Ireland, microfilm Pos 934, Neg 852, referred to below simply as 'passenger list') and various lists in the Provincial Archives of New Brunswick relating to the *Star*.

Code to surname references below:
a) Townland as spelt in the Emigration Books in the Fitzwilliam Papers, National Library of Ireland. Ref: MS 4974 & 4975.
b) Official spelling of the townland.
c) Civil parish in which the townland is situated.
d) Reference number in the Emigration Book
e) Group members, ages, and relationships
f) Description of holding on the Fitzwilliam estate
g) Other information

BAIN, Thomas 22. Travelled with his sister and brother-in-law, Mary and John Popham. See below.

BALANCE (a) Coolfancy (b) Coolafancy (c) Crosspatrick (d) 67 (e) John 27, wife Anty 26, son William 18 months, mother-in-law Rose Waddock 57, brother-in-law Pat Waddock 35. (f) Cabin from Mrs Pearce. (g) On passenger list William Waddock was also named.

BEAGHEN (a) Urelands (b) Newry (c) Moyacomb (d) 60 (e)Thomas 45, wife Mary 44, children John 26, James 24, Margaret 22, Catherine 20, Mary 18, Pat 16, Thomas 14, Andy 12, James' wife Mary 24 & daughter Anty 9 months. (f) Cabin from Mr Hope. (g) This family first listed for emigration in 1847. Ref: 1, they then had a cabin & half-acre from Hope. House to come down. They are also on the passenger list.

BOULGER (a) Tubberpatrick (b) Toberpatrick (c) Kilpipe (d) 140 (e) John

50, wife Alice 46, children Dorothy 23, James 21, Thomas 19, Edward 13, Eliza 8, Francis 6, Tempey(?) 3. Son-in-law Peter Carroll 25, (married to Dorothy?) grandson John 3 weeks. (Some confusion with Peter Carroll, see of Tubberpatrick below). (f) Cabin on Dowse farm. (g) On passenger list.

BYRNE (a) Coolelug (b) Coolalug (c) Kilpipe (d) 133 (e) James 46, wife Ann 44, children Margaret 20, Hugh 18, Pat 16, Daniel 13, James 11, Thomas 10. (f) Cabin from Charles Byrne. (g) On passenger list.

BYRNE (a) Kilballyowen (b) Kilballyowen (c) Preban (d) 27 (e) John 40, wife Bridget 40, children Thomas 15, Anne 6, Betty 4. (f) Cabin from Mrs Mary Kavanagh. (g) On passenger list.

BYRNE (a) Kilballyowen (b) Kilballyowen (c) Preban (d) 28 (e) John 34, wife Mary 34, children Jno. 7, Biddy 5, James 4, Pat 18 months. (f) Cabin from Peter Kingston. (g) This family on passenger list, his sister Bridget appears on this list but not in the Emigration Book.

BYRNE (a) Kilcaven (b) Kilcavan (c) Carnew (d) 144 (e) James 44, wife Anne 40, children Simon 19, Sally 18, Biddy 16, Margaret 14, Kitty 12, Bess 10, James 8, Anne 6. (f) House and 6.5 acres from Lord Fitzwilliam. (g) This family on passenger list.

BYRNE (a) Killaveny (b) Killaveny (c) Kilpipe (d) 17 (e) John 40, wife Sarah 32, children Elizabeth 15, James 12, Margaret 9, John William 3. (f) Cabin and 1 acre from Jno. Dowzer (Dowse?). (g) This family on passenger list.

BYRNE (a) Kilpipe/Coolbawn (b) Kilpipe (c) Kilpipe (d) 52 (e) Matthew 53, wife Rose 46 Andrew 20, Pat 17, Honoria 15, James 14, Ellen 12, Daniel 10, Matt 8, Greg 6. (f) House & 32 acres on John Byrne's holding under ejectment. (g) On passenger list, with the addition of Mary 22.

BYRNE(a) Munny (b) Money (c) Aghowle (d) 36 (e) Mary 62, children Simon 26, Betty 24, Michael 30, John 22. (f) Cabin & 3 roods from James Carroll. (g) This family listed in 1847 Emigration Book (ref 251) but not in 1848.

BYRNE (a) Munny (b) Money (c) Aghowle (d) 31 (e) Joseph 55, wife Nancy 56, children Biddy 28, Michael 26, Judith 22, Hugh 18. (f) Cabin from Capt Nickson. 'Mick Loughlin attended here and stated he would pull down Byrne's house.' (g) First listed in 1847 ref 66 passenger list.

BYRNE (a) Munny (b) Money (c) Aghowle (d) 91 (e) John 35, wife Mary 28, children Simon 12, Peter 6, Kitty 8, Daniel 3; his brothers Patrick 48, James 35. (f) Cabin from Richard Codd. (g) On passenger list.

BYRNE (a) Tubberpatrick (b) Toberpatrick (c) Kilpipe (d) 119 (e) John 56 (66?), wife Bridget 75(?), children James 36, Dolly 25, James' wife Rose 30 & sons James 6, Pat 1. Dolly's husband Peter Carroll 36 and their son John 1 month (there seems to be a mix-up in the Emigration book, as this Peter Carroll is also listed with Boulger family above. (f) Cabin & 12 acres from Lord Fitzwilliam. On passenger list.

CAFFREY (a) Tubberpatrick (b) Toberpatrick (c) Kilpipe (d) 72 (e) Michael 30, wife Mary 30, children Anne 15, Esty 13, Kitty 11, Eliza 9, Jane 7, Phil 5, Ellen 3. (f) Cabin from Jno. Brownrigg. (g) Jane died on voyage. On passenger list.

CALL (a) Muchlagh (b) Mucklagh (c) Kilpipe (d) 4 (e) Jno. 40, wife Biddy 30, children James 14, Francis 12, Lawrence 8, Margo 1. (f) Cabin from Charles Byrne. (g) On passenger list.

CARROLL Peter. See Boulger of Tubberpatrick and Byrne of Tubberpatrick.

CLARE, John. See Catherine Kavanagh, Kilcaven.

CODD (a) Munny (b) Money (c) Aghowle (d) 51 (e) John 33, wife Sarah 30, daughter Margaret 2; brother. William 25, sister Jane 22, cousin John Codd 21. (f) Cabin from Captain Nickson. Has given up his land. (g) On passenger list.

CONNERIN (a) Rasnastraw (b) Rosnastraw (c) Kilpipe (d) 24 (e) Betty 50, children Jno. 23, Catherine 25, Betty 16, James 14; brother-in-law Jno. Dempsey 33 & his son James Dempsey 2. (f) Cabin fron Jno. New. (g) All on passenger list.

CULLEN (a) Coolroe (b) Coolroe (c) Crosspatrick (d) 87 (e) Patrick 38, wife Ellen 40, children James 16, Michael 11. (f) Cabin and kitchen garden from James Griffin. (g) On passenger list.

DEMPSEY, Jno. See Connerin of Rasnastraw above.

DOWNS (a) Gurteen/Greenhall (b) Gorteen (c) Crosspatrick (d) 20 (e) Daniel 40, wife Mary 40, children Anne 15, Eliza 12, Kate 9, Mary 6, Michael 3. (f) Cabin and 2 acres from John James. (g) On passenger list.

DOYLE (a) Mucklagh (b) Mucklagh (c) Kilpipe (d) 7 (e) John 30, wife Catherine 35, children Mary 7, Jno. 4, Pat 18 months; sister Sarah 23. (f) Cabin & kitchen garden from Charles Byrne. (g) On passenger list.

DOYLE (a) Ballagh (b) Ballagh (c) Kilpipe (d) 30 (e) Jno. 23, wife Bridget 22, daughter Peggy 2.5 years; brother Daniel 21, sister Mary 18, neither will go. (f) Cabin & 2 acres from the late Thomas Smith's holding now in the possession of Mrs Pearse. (g) On passenger list.

FALLON (a) Boley (b) Boley (c) Aghowle (d) 77 (e) Margaret 25, sister Bridget 22 (f) Cabin from James Keeley. To come down. (g) On passenger list.

FARRELL (a) Barrenbaum (b) ? (c) ? (d) 149 (e) William 31, wife ? 30; James ??? 28 (f) Cabin from John Brangan. (g) On passenger list, which also mentions two infants.

FOLEY (a) Urelands (b) Newry (c) Moyacomb (d) 61 (e) Denis 37, wife Bridget 24, children John 6, Derbis 4, Mary 3 (f) Cabin from Mr Hope. Mr Challoner has consented to let this house stand. (g) Denis died on voyage. First listed for emigration in 1847. Not on passenger list.

FOX (a) Ballinulta (b) Ballynultagh (c) Mullinacuffe (d) 98 (e) Patrick 38, wife Bess 37, children John 18, Susan 15, Henry 13, ? 11, Mary Ellen 6. (f) Cabin from Joseph Griffin. (g) On passenger list.

FURLONG (a) Ballard (b) Ballard (c) Aghowle (d) 18 (e) Michael 47, wife Elizabeth 37, children Anne 17, Mary 15, Bridget 13, Eliza 11, Essy 8, Catherine 6, Hannah 4; and Margaret Healy 19, a relative. (f) House & 21 acres from Lord Fitzwilliam. (g) Michael died at St Andrews on 5 June, 1848. On passenger list.

GAHAN (a) Farnees (b) Farnees (c) Kilcommon (d) 70 (e) John 42, wife Ann 38, children George 21. (f) 7 acres from Mrs Leonard. (g) On passenger list.

GIDDENS (a) Ballagh (b) Ballagh (c) Kilpipe (d) 14 (e) James 27, wife Mary 26, children John 2; brother George 28, sister Ellen 18. (f) Cabin and kitchen garden from Robert Smith. (g) On passenger list.

HUGHES (a) Lascoleman (b) Liscolman (c) Liscolman (d) 130 (e) Robert 38, wife Margaret 38, children Mary 13, Mick 11, Kitty 9, Pat 6, John 4, James 1. (f) Cabin & half-acre from James Kennedy. (g) All on passenger list except James.

HUGHES, Thomas, See Neal of Knockeen below.

HYLAND (a) Lascoleman (b) Liscolman (c) Liscolman (d) 108 (e) John 64, wife Catherine 58, children Pat 22, John 17, Catherine 19, David 15, James 13, Ellen 11. (f) Cabin from Edward Bourke. (g) On passenger list. First listed for emigration in 1847, reference 246.

JONES (a) Ballicioniogue (b) Ballyshonog (c) Kilcommon (d) 29 (e) Richard 40, wife Mazzy 35, children Jane 17, Margaret 15, Mary 13, Thomas 12, John 10, Richard 6, Pat 2. (f) Cabin & 6.5 acres from Messrs. Bates & Morton's holding. (g) On passenger list.

KAVANAGH (a) Kilcaven (b) Kilcavan (c) Carnew (d) 137 (e) Catherine 60, children Johannah 33, Walter 30, Mary 20. Johannah's husband John Clare 33, children, Bridget 8, Mary 2, Pat 4. (f) Cabin & 10 acres. Query will John Clare go? (g) All, including John Clare, appear on passenger list.

KEALY/KEELEY (a) Lascoleman (b) Liscolman (c) Liscolman (d) 81 (e) Daniel 60, wife Catherine 57, children Anne 36, Mick 30, Mary 22, John 20, Catherine 18. (f) Cabin from Jno. Sheppard. (g) Daniel died at St Andrews on 7 June 1848. On passenger list, Anne not on this list but Mick's wife Bridget 27 is. Also in 1847 Emigration Book, reference 2. See Mulhall of Lascoleman below.

KELLY (a) Farnees (b) Farnees (c) Kilcommon (d) 10 (e) James 34, wife Margaret 28, children John 11, Ruth 9, James 6, Margaret 4. (f) Cabin & kitchen garden from Mrs Leonard. (g) Margaret jnr (Peg) died on voyage. Also in 1847 Emigration Book, ref 17. Mrs Leonard was concerned about their place of destination but no details are given. On passenger list.

KERWAN (a) Munney (b) Money (c) Aghowle (d) 102 (e) Mary 50, children Morgan 31, Pat 29, Margaret 27, Eliza 25, Catherine 23, Judy 21. Grandson James 9 months. (f) Cabin from James Carroll. (g) Also in 1847 Emigration Book ref 26, perhaps delayed for birth of James. On passenger list. Grandson down as Pat Morgan and Morgan not mentioned, – obviously a mix-up.

KERWAN (a) Tubberlonagh (b) Toberlownagh (c) Kilpipe (d) 1 (e) David 26, wife Catherine 21, sister Catherine 22 (f) Cabin in yard of Farrell Keoghoe which he holds rent free. (g) On passenger list, which includes David's sisters Sarah 29 and Margaret 25.

LAWLER (a) Park (b) Drummin (c) Moyacomb (d) 8 e() Thomas 55, wife Ellen 45, children Ann 24, John 22, James 18, Peter 17, Ellen 14, Mary 11, Thomas 7, Betty 4. (f) Cabin & kitchen garden from William Hopkins. g) On passenger list.

McCANN (a) Minmore (b) Minmore (c) Carnew (d) 173 (e) John 66, wife Betty 53, children George 23, Margaret 25, Mary 23, Eliza 18, Eliza (again) 19, Anne 15, John 13. (f) Cabin from Elizabeth Twamley. Not on passenger list. Also in 1847 Emigration Book ref 90 in which Michael 19 appears instead of second Eliza.

McDANIEL (a) Kilballyowen (b) Kilballyowen (c) Preban (d) 13 (e)

Francis 40, wife Ellen 40, children Mary 20, Ellen 18, Terence 16, Tom 14, Peter 12, Pat 10, James 8, John 6, Frank 4; Frank's mother Ellen 60. (f) Cabin & 3 acres from Mary Kavanagh. (g) This family appears as McDonnell in the New Brunswick records. Young Frank died on voyage. Peter & Terry died within 3 days of each other in St Andrews. On passenger list.

MEAGHER (a) Coolfancy (b) Coolafancy (c) Crosspatrick (d) 68 (e) Thomas 35, wife Ann 26, children Ellen 6, Pat 4, Mary 2, sister Catherine 18, brother John 20 – 'query as they do be at service'. (f) Cabin & kitchen garden from Joseph Gilbert. (g) Ellen died at St Andrews on 31 May 1848. All, except Mary 2, on passenger list.

MOONEY (a) Knockeen (b) Knockeen (c) Liscolman (d) 88 (e) Mary 60, children John 32, Michael 30, Paul 28, Peter 26, James 24. (f) Cabin & kitchen garden from Jno. Cummins. House to come down. (g) On passenger list. See also 1847 Emigration Book reference 220.

MOULTS (a) Tankersley (b) ? (c) ? (d) 56 (e) William 48, wife Catherine 44, children Margaret 24, James 22, Robert 19, William 16, Anne 13, Catherine 9. (f) Cabin & 2 acres from Mr Coates. (g) On passenger list.

MULHALL (a) Lascoleman (b) Liscolman (c) Liscolman (d) 81 (e) Thomas 30, wife Bridget, children Catherine 7, Mary 5, infant Thomas. (f) No details (g) Travelled with Kealy/Keeley of Lascoleman above. On passenger list. Also on this is Ann 3. See also Emigration Book for 1847 reference 2.

NEAL (a) Killaveny (b) Killaveny (c) Kilpipe (d) 59 (e) Peggy 54, children James 23, Andy 20, Mick 16, Margaret 14, Mary 28, Betty 22, Polly 21, Biddy 24. (f) Cabin from Jno. Neill. On passenger list.

NEALE (a) Killaveny (b) Killaveny (c) Kilpipe (d) 3 (e) James 20, brothers John 17, Denis 14; sisters Ann 28, Catherine 23 Mary 11. (f) Cabin & 5 acres from Jno. O'Neill. g) On passenger list.

NEIL (a) Killaveny (b) Killaveny (c) Kilpipe (d) 101 (e) Laurence 48, wife Anne 36, son James 6; brother Denis 36 & Denis' wife Margaret 26 & son Denis 6. (f) All on passenger list.

NEIL (a) Knockeen (b) Knockeen (c) Liscolman (d) None (e) John 35, wife Catherine 26, son Pat 2. Thomas Hughes 26 (f) No trace of this family in Fitzwilliam Emigration Books, this information is from the passenger list.

NOWLAN (a) Militia (b) Moylisha (c) Moyacomb (d) 42 (e) Pat 50, wife Betty 38, children Peggy 20, James 18, Mary 17, Mick 16, John 14, Ellen 13, Martin 9, Biddy 7. (f) House and 5 acres from Mr Brownrigg. g) On passenger list with slight mix-up in names.

OWENS (a) Farnees (b) Farnees (c) Kilcommon (d) 40 (e) John 20; sisters Mary 22, Kitty 16, Anne 14, Eliza 12; brother Edward 18 (f) Cabin & 5 acres from Mrs Leonard. (g) On passenger list.

POPHAM (a) Munny (b) Money (c) Aghowle (d)15 (e) John 28, wife Mary 30, children Sarah 4, Abey 2, Thomas 1; brother-in-law Thomas Bain 22. (f) Cabin & kitchen garden from Captain Nickson. (g) On passenger list. This family appears as Poppin in New Brunswick records.

PRESTLEY (a) Killaveny (b) Killaveny (c) Kilpipe (d) 129 (e) Pat 27, wife Sally 20, son Andy 1, brother Mick 25. (f) Cabin & 10 acres from Jno. Neill. (g) On passenger list.

SUMMERS (a) Urelands (b) Newry (c) Moyacomb (d) 147 (e) John 50, wife Betty 50, children Michael 24, Marks 22, James 20, John 18, Thomas 16, Pat 14, Eliza 12, Ally 10. (f) 3.5 acres and cottage from Mr Dowse. House to come down. (g) On passenger list.

STEDMAN (a) Killballyowen (b) Killballyowen (c) Preban (d) 38 (e) John 42, wife Mary 43, children Thomas 23, Pat 21, Biddy 16, Dolly 13. (f) Cabin and half-rood from Doyle's farm under ejectment. (g) On passenger list.

TOOLE (a) Killaveny (b) Killaveny (c) Kilpipe (d) 69 (e) Bart 50, wife Anne 48, children Thomas 24, Bess 21, Judy 18, Mary 17, Ann 14, James 12, Ellen 10, John 8. (f) Cabin & kitchen garden from Mr Dowzer (Dowse?) (g) On passenger list.

WADDOCK See Balance of Coolfancy above

WELSH (a) Killaveny (b) Killaveny (c) Kilpipe (d) 25 (e) Michael 49, wife Mary 52, children Thomas 24, Peter 21, Michael 18, Mary 15. (f) Cabin from Charles Willoughby. g) On passenger list.

WHITE (a) Coolfancy (b) Coolafancy (c) Crosspatrick (d) 9 (e) David 37, wife Ann 37, children Edward 14, Richard 10, Henry 6, Ann 1; brother Robert White 40. (f) Cabin & kitchen garden from William White. On passenger list but Edward not mentioned and Margaret 14 and Andrews 10 added. David died on voyage.

Appendix 2

Townland populations in 1841, 1851 and 1861, and the numbers of individuals cleared from those townlands between 1847 and 1850, and 1851 and 1856.

Townland	Census 1841	Cleared 1847–50	Census 1851	Cleared 1851–56	Census 1861
Aghowle	422	80	288	48	191
Ardoyne	307	58	248	2	222
Askakeagh	203	57	94	37	49
Balisland	146	6	86	10	76
Ballagh	109	33	70	0	49
Ballard	64	62	30	27	20
Ballinacorbeg	201	9	140	0	86
Ballingate	396	33	310	7	233
Ballinglen	222	6	177	14	124
Ballinguile	292	107	187	71	134
Ballybeg	139	19	76	5	58
Ballyconnell	326	39	244	0	186
Ballycumber	206	19	135	0	99
Ballykelly	178	19	126	64	54
Ballinavortha	43	0	48	9	47
Ballynultagh	621	282	349	106	222
Ballyrahan	204	86	180	33	142
Ballyshonog	172	26	112	20	75
Ballyvolan	119	8	127	0	63
Barrenbawn	75	9	62	9	37
Boley	260	78	135	10	112
Burkeen	31	9	9	0	13
Carnew	1,435	51	1,188	3	1,056
Carrignamweel	127	13	91	9	33
Carrigroe	99	21	61	16	38
Coolafancy	392	173	238	52	160
Coolafunshoge	133	0	116	7	86
Coolalug	129	17	59	4	55
Coolattin	349	124	268	95	189
Coolbawn	196	10	162	0	127
Coolboy	300	123	192	28	124

Coolkenna	391	51	258	0	234
Coolroe	405	107	262	27	197
Coolruss			unidentified		
Corndog	73	8	39	19	15
Cronelea	130	76	48	12	38
Croneyhorn	380	50	259	0	258
Curravanish	94	0	90	5	71
Drummin			unidentified		
Farnees	147	50	100	37	82
Glasgarnet	46	4	34	0	209
Glenphillippeen	122	47	79	52	35
Gorteen	83	50	53	1	32
Gowle	152	45	85	8	65
Greenhall	36	0	11	1	6
Hillbrook	211	141	104	2	89
Kilcavan	255	134	155	9	121
Killabeg	220	43	170	19	98
Killaveny	388	61	249	3	219
Killballyowen	490	88	277	23	191
Killinure	618	220	358	69	274
Kilmalone			unidentified		
Kilpipe	144	36	110	11	111
Kilquiggin	194	61	128	35	186
Knockatomcoyle	384	44	241	30	194
Knockeen	202	34	175	0	124
Knockloe	92	45	59	5	65
Knocknaboley	235	22	174	40	130
Laragh	82	22	41	15	36
Leighlin			unidentified		
Liscolman	276	49	215	0	165
Lugduff	103	21	133	9	110
Mangans	86	0	67	7	59
Minmore	78	55	47	8	42
Money	321	90	240	0	178
Moylisha	162	45	80	5	80
Moyne	94	0	103	9	77
Mucklagh	185	20	125	12	79
Mullannaskeagh	36	22	10	0	9
Mullans	197	42	106	54	75
Mungacullen	150	27	125	0	96

Muskeagh	109	0	71	24	57
Newcastle	447	15	296	0	244
Newtown	159	0	82	8	77
Newry	255	92	166	0	133
Park	92	7	72	0	61
Parkmore	123	0	60	21	36
Paulbeg	62	16	50	0	21
Raheengraney	178	23	151	0	113
Rath	5	8	3	0	7
Rathbane	151	32	97	0	96
Rathcot	34	0	38	8	35
Rathmeague	87	4	59	33	49
Rathshanmore	183	131	120	0	108
Roddenagh	120	13	43	2	26
Rosbane	179	88	102	24	74
Rosnakill					
Rosnastraw	239	36	163	0	142
Slievemweel	211	59	99	11	64
Slievenamough	129	103	62	24	61
Slieveroe	141	35	111	24	82
Stranakelly	200	27	132	0	132
Tallyhoe			unidentified		
Tankersley			unidentified		
Tanseyclose	20	5	15	0	13
Tinahely	661	12	575	0	536
Toberlownagh	128	10	92	0	98
Toberpatrick	244	59	145	0	11
Tomacork	205	13	112	13	105
Tombreen	332	40	228	48	164
Tomcoyle	74	0	27	8	22
Tomnafinnoge	213	25	139	15	130
Tomnaskeale	77	0	83	12	38
Toorboy	62	35	49	0	28
Tullowclay	90	11	84	0	63
Umrygar	78	6	70	0	67
TOTALS	20,446	4,292	14,014	1,488	11,209

APPENDIX 3
DUNBRODY

One of the principal ships used in the Fitzwilliam Clearances was the *Dunbrody*, owned by Graves & Son of New Ross. In 1993 work began on construction of a full-sized replica of this vessel and this is now nearing completion. The project was initiated by the J.F. Kennedy Trust because of the close ties between the region of New Ross and that family. J.F. Kennedy's ancestor sailed from there during the period covered in this book.

The original *Dunbrody* was built in Quebec in 1845. A barque rigged vessel of 458 tons, she was a typical example of the type of ship used in the famine emigration trade. Her replica is now moored in New Ross at the same quay from which the Fitzwilliam emigrants sailed, giving her many visitors an awareness of what crossing the Atlantic meant in those distant days.

The Visitor Centre is open seven days a week and there are audio-visual facilities, a guided tour, and free parking. For more information contact:

John F. Kennedy Trust
New Ross, Co. Wexford, Ireland
Phone: 051 425239 Fax:051 425240
e-mail:jfktrust@iol.ie
www.dunbrody.com

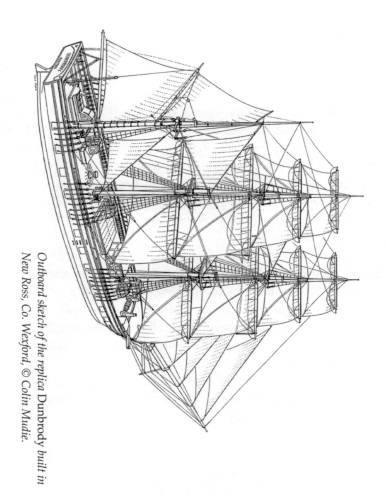

Outboard sketch of the replica Dunbrody built in New Ross, Co. Wexford, © Colin Mudie.

Appendix 4

Database
The Fitzwilliam Estate Clearances 1847–1856

The names of all the Fitzwilliam tenants who went to Canada or Australia as part of the 1847–56 clearance programme were entered in the estate's Emigration Books. The entries were made in chronological order and were not indexed. This meant that if a researcher were looking for a particular family, it would be necessary to go through all the names until the correct entry was found. This information has now been computerised and is accessible in full (that is, for *all* the people named in the Emigration Books and just those of the *Star*) on the County Wicklow Heritage website (www. countywicklowheritage.org/page_id__45_path__0p3p.aspx) and the portal page of the Provincial Archives of New Brunswick website (archives.gnb.ca/Irish/exhibits_en.html).

What information does it contain?

The census (for that is what the Emigration Books are) lists full names, ages, family groupings, townlands of origin – spelled as they appear in the ledgers as well as the official version – the civil parish, original manuscript reference number, and year of emigration. Many entries also include the ports and dates of departure and arrival, the names of the ships, and miscellaneous remarks about the size of the holding surrendered (whether a cabin or, as in one case, a 170-acre farm). In some cases the inducement to quit the estate was recorded. This was usually 'Passage & Support'. Support could mean anything from 10 shillings a head to a single cash settlement. Others had their rent arrears written off.

A typical entry is as follows:

Surname:	Owens
Townland (as in ms):	Farnees
Townland (official):	Farnees
Civil Parish:	Kilcommon

Surplus People

Year:	1848
Ms ref no:	40
Father (age):	John 20
Mother (age):	None
Children:	None
Others:	Sisters Mary 22, Kitty 16, Anne 14, Eliza 12; brother Edward 18.
Ship:	*Star*
Port & date of departure:	New Ross, April 1848
Port & date of arrival:	St Andrews, June 1848
Miscellaneous:	Cabin and 5 acres from Mrs Leonard, a head tenant. House to come down.
No. of people in group:	6

For further information
Jim Rees, 3 Meadows Lane, Arklow, Co. Wicklow, Ireland
tel: 353 402 39125 fax: 353 402 39064
e-mail: jrees@eircom.net

ENDNOTES

Abbreviations
FP: The Fitzwilliam Papers
ms: Manuscript
NAI: National Archives of Ireland
NLI: National Library of Ireland
PANB: Provincial Archives of New Brunswick
PLC: Poor Law Commission Papers
RCP: Relief Commission Papers
WHR: Waterford Harbour Records

Introduction
1. Christine Kinealy, *This Great Calamity: The Irish Famine 1845–52* (Dublin 1994).
2. Ken Hannigan 'Wicklow Before and After The Famine' and Eva Ó Cathaoir: 'The Poor Law in County Wicklow' essays in *Wicklow History and Society* (Dublin 1994).
3. Hannigan, *op.cit.*
4. For the full story of this emigration see Jim Rees, *A Farewell To Famine*, 2nd ed. Dee-Jay Publications (Arklow, 1995).

Chapter 1: Coolattin Estate
1. The county of Wicklow was not established until 1606. Up to that time the region was variously known as 'O Byrne Countrie' or was lumped into one of the adjoining counties, in this case Dublin.
2. P. Lennon, 'Eighteenth-century landscape change from estate records – Coolattin estate, Shillelagh, county Wicklow', B.A. geography dissertation, TCD (1979), pp 5–6.
3. G.E.C: *The Complete Peerage* (London 1926).
4. FP, NLI, ms 4948 – Memoranda dealing with tenancies 1796–1841.
5. *The Complete Peerage*.
6. Ibid, p 524

Chapter 2: Life on the Coolattin Estate:1830–1845
1. FP, NLI, ms 4948, 1832/33 item 13.
2. Ibid, 1837 item 10.

3. Ibid, 1832/33 item 15.

4. Ibid, 1832/33 item 14.

5. Ibid. ms 3993

6. Ibid. ms 4948. There are many instances of such agreements in the memoranda.

7. Ibid, 1836 item 49.

8. Ibid. ms 4973, p222. The same page shows Ralph Lawrenson, a leading man on the estate, earning £200 p.a.

9. Ibid, 1836 item 28.

10. Ibid, 1832/33 item 1.

11. Ken Hannigan 'Wicklow Before and After the Famine' in *Wicklow History and Society* (Dublin 1994), p797.

12. PLC 1836, Vol XXXI, Appendix D. NAI.

13. FP, NLI, ms 4948. See also mss 3989, 3909, 4973, 4966, 4948. Many instances recorded.

14. Ibid.

15. Ibid. ms 4962 *Poor Shop Book* 1830–38.

16. Ibid, 1842 item 5.

17. Letter to Jim Rees from Joe Hayden a resident in the Killaveny district.

18. Eva Ó Cathaoir: 'The Poor Law in County Wicklow' in *Wicklow History and Society* (Dublin 1994) p503.

19 FP, NLI, ms 4963

20. FP, NLI, ms 4948, 1831 item 15.

21. Ibid, 1842 item 4.

Chapter 3: The Poor Law

1. Edmund Burke, *Thoughts and Details on Scarcity* (London 1795).

2. May be related to Thomas Whateley who had been co-draughtsman of the English Poor Law.

3. Christine Kinealy, *This Great Calamity: The Irish Famine 1845–52* (Dublin 1994) p 307.

4. Eva Ó Cathaoir, *op.cit.* p. 523

5. For a full account of the Poor Law in County Wicklow see Eva Ó Cathaoir's paper in the above note.

6. Ibid. p 506. See also footnote 12, p. 570.

7. FP, NLI, ms 4948, 1841 item 12.

Endnotes

Chapter 4: Crisis: 1845–1846

1. Cormac Ó Gráda, *Ireland before and after the famine: Explorations in Economic History 1800–1925* (Manchester, 1988), p. 51.
2. RCP, NAI, II/2B 5878.
3. Ibid. 5829.
4. Ken Hannigan, *op.cit.*
5. RCP II/2A/11008, NAI.

Chapter 5: Shedding the Surplus

1. FP, NLI, mss 4974, 4975. There were several instances of comments such as 'Will not go' written beside names in the ledgers.
2. Ibid 4974.
3. Ibid 4975. See entry for Anne Lynch 1853.
4. *Illustrated London News*, May 1851.

Chapter 6: Life in the 'Tween Decks

1. I am grateful to Denis Noel of the Provincial Archives of New Brunswick for copies of the relevant Passenger Acts. Examples of breaches of these acts litter the pages of contemporary newspapers.
2. Charbonneau, Andre & Sevigny, Andre, *1847 Grosse Île: a Record of Daily Events*, (Ottawa 1997), p. 50.

Chapter 7: Quebec

1. McQuillan, D. Aidan, *The Irish in Quebec*, p 263.
2. These and subsequent statistics of ships arriving at Grosse Île in 1847 are taken from two recently published books: Marianna O'Gallagher and Rose Masson Dompierre, *Eyewitness – Grosse Île 1847*, Livres Carraig Books, 1995; Andre Charbonneau and Andre Sevigny, *1847 Grosse Île: A Record of Daily Events*, Canadian Heritage, Parks Canada, 1997.
3. O'Gallagher & Dompierre, *op. cit.* p 6.
4. Ibid. p 52.
5. Charbonneau & Sevigny, *op.cit.* p 60.
6. O'Gallagher & Dompierre, *op. cit.* p 84.
7. Papers Relative to Emigration, HC, 1848, vol.47, G.M. Douglas, MD, to Hon. D. Daly (provincial secretary) dated 27 December 1847, being a report on the year at Grosse Île. (As quoted in *Passage To America,* Terry Coleman, Penguin Books edition 1974, reprinted 1976. p 173.)
8. James J. Mangan (Ed.), *Robert Whyte's 1847 Famine Ship Diary,* Mercier Press, 1994. p 73.

9. Peter Shawn Taylor, 'Ancestral Trail', *Canadian Geographic* Jan–Feb 1996. pp 38–46.

10. O'Gallagher & Dompierre, *op.cit.* pp 195–196.

11. Collard, Edgar A, *Montreal – The Days That Are No More*, Totem Books; Toronto 1976. p 123.

12. Ibid. p 124

13. FP, NLI, ms 4975

Chapter 8: New Brunswick

1. I am grateful to Gail G. Campbell and Ruth Bleasdale of St Thomas' University in Fredericton, New Brunswick for allowing me access to the results of their research into this railroad.

2. *New Brunswick Courier*, 10 July 1847.

3. Special Report from Asa Coy, Esquire, in reference to Emigrants at St Andrews, Legislative Assembly of New Brunswick, Sessional papers (1850), Appendix.

4. FP, NLI, ms 3987, p204.

5. Ibid. neg 582, pos 934.

6. Ibid. ms 4975.

7. WHR (Arrivals 1848), NAI. New Ross was an outport of Waterford and details of arrivals and departures were recorded as part of the larger port's activities.

8. FP, NLI, ms 3987, p216.

9. PANB, RS9 1848-07-06 #33.1, f17923.

10. Ibid.

11. This is confusing because Hospital Island and Quarantine Island are generally regarded as being the same piece of land. Contemporary and modern sources reflect this. It is possible that Boyd used one of the neighbouring islands as a temporary quarantine but this is the only reference which indicates two different islands. I am particularly grateful to local historian George Haney for his advice on this point.

12. PANB, RS555 B2b3, pp 674–677.

13. Ibid. pp 617–618.

14. Ibid. pp 629–630.

15. This was a levy on shipowners or their agents so that the the total costs of maintaining destitute immigrants would not fall on the recipient community.

16. PANB, RS555 B2b3, pp 632–635.

17. Ibid. pp 642–644.

18. Ibid. pp 650–653.

19. Ibid. pp 654–656.

20. See note 2 above.

21. PANB, RS555, p662, dated 23 June 1848.

22. Ibid. no number, 27 July 1848.

23. PANB, RG4, RS24, 1848/pe 4 – as quoted in Note 1 above.

24. PANB, RS637, 7d7a3

25. PANB, Hill Collection MC10001-MS318. Letter from Wilson to Hill, dated October 3rd, 1848, expressing optimism of attracting 'good men to settle on the line, say English and Scotchmen who have some capital'.

26. PANB, RS555, 12 September 1848.

27. FP, NLI, ms 3987, p223, dated 18 July 1848.

28. Ibid. p226, dated 26 August 1848.

29. PANB, Hill Collection MC1001-MS318. Dated 3 October 1848.

30. PANB, RS555 B2b3, p608, dated 2 January 1849.

31. Ibid. pp 674–677, dated 15 January 1849.

32. Ibid.

33. As Note 1.

34. PANB, RS555 B2b3, p608, dated 2 January 1849.

35. Asa Coy's report, *op.cit.*

36. PANB, RS555, B2b3, pp 964–965, dated 26 January 1849.

37. Ibid. not numbered, dated January 1849.

38. PANB, RS346L.

39. PANB, RS555, B2b3, not numbered, dated 4 April 1849.

40. Ibid. not numbered, dated 7 May 1849.

41. My thanks to Gail Nightingale of Veazes, Maine, a descendant of the Thomas Mulhall for this information.

42. See Note 1, p 23.

43. *The History of McAdam 1871–1977*. PANB MC80/429.

44. I.M. McQuinn, 'Histories of the Railways of the province of New Brunswick' PANB MC80/215.

45. FP, NLI, ms 4975.

Chapter 9: 1850–6

1. According to Graves' advertisement, Captain Williams was in charge.

2. WHR (Arrivals 1850), NAI.

3. My thanks to Jean Broadfoot of Ottawa for arrival dates of these vessels at Quebec.

4. It is still common practice to refer to New Ross simply as Ross.

5. As note 3.

6. Further amendments to the Passenger Acts had been passed into legislation in 1852.

BIBLIOGRAPHY

BOOKS

Burke, Edmund, *Thoughts and Details on Scarcity,* (London 1795).

Charbonneau, André & Sevigny, André, *1847 Grosse Île: a Record of Daily Events,* (Ottawa 1997).

Coleman, Terry, *Passage To America,* Penguin Books edition 1974, reprinted 1976.

Collard, Edgar A, *Montreal – The Days That Are No More,* (Toronto 1976)

G.E.C: *The Complete Peerage,* (London 1926).

Hannigan & Nolan (eds), *Wicklow History & Society,* (Dublin 1994).

I.M. McQuinn, *Histories of the Railways of the Province of New Brunswick,* Photocopy, Provincial Archives of New Brunswick MC80/215.

Kinealy, Christine, *This Great Calamity:The Irish Famine 1845–52,* (Dublin 1994).

Mangan, James J. (Ed.), *Robert Whyte's 1847 Famine Ship Diary,* (Cork, 1994).

McQuillan, D Aidan, *The Irish in Quebec.*

Ó Gráda, Cormac, *Ireland before and after the famine: Explorations in Economic History 1800–1925,* (Manchester, 1988).

Rees, Jim, *A Farewell To Famine* (Arklow, 1995).

O'Gallagher, Marianna & Dompierre, Rose Masson, *Eyewitness – Grosse Île 1847* (Quebec 1995).

MANUSCRIPTS

FITZWILLIAM PAPERS, HELD IN THE NATIONAL LIBRARY OF IRELAND
mss 3909, 3987, 3989, 3993, 4948, 4962, 4963, 4966, 4973, 4974, 4975
microfilm neg 582, pos 934.

PAPERS RELATING TO THE SHIP *STAR*, HELD IN THE PROVINCIAL ARCHIVES OF NEW BRUNSWICK:
ms Hill Collection MC10001-MS318.
microfilm, RS9 1848-07-06 #33.1, f17923, RS555 B2b3, RS637, 7d7a3, RG4, RS24, RS346L.
printed, *The History of McAdam* 1871–1977 MC80/429.

M<small>ISCELLANEOUS</small>

Campbell, Gail G. and Bleasdale, Ruth, of St Thomas' University in Fredericton, New Brunswick. Their paper on the St Andrews–Quebec Railway is to be published shortly.

Lennon, P, 'Eighteenth century landscape change from estate records – Coolattin estate, Shillelagh, county Wicklow', B.A. geography dissertation, TCD (1979).

Lloyd's register of Shipping, 1847–1856.

Taylor, Peter Shawn, 'Ancestral Trail', *Canadian Geographic* Jan–Feb 1996. pp 38–46.

N<small>EWSPAPERS</small>
Illustrated London News.
New Brunswick Courier.
Wexford Independent.

O<small>FFICIAL</small> R<small>EPORTS AND</small> P<small>UBLICATIONS</small>
N<small>ATIONAL</small> A<small>RCHIVES OF</small> I<small>RELAND</small>
Devon Commission Report.
Poor Law Commission Papers 1836, Vol XXXI, Appendix D.
Relief Commission Papers, II/2B 5878, and II/2A/11008.
Waterford Harbour Records Arrivals 1848 and Arrivals 1850.

P<small>ROVINCIAL</small> A<small>RCHIVES OF</small> N<small>EW</small> B<small>RUNSWICK</small>
British Passenger Acts 1803–1852.
Special Report from *Asa Coy, Esquire, in reference to Emigrants at St Andrews*, Legislative Assembly of New Brunswick, Sessional papers (1850).

INDEX

For names of passengers who sailed on the ship *Star*, see Appendix 1. Some of these names will also be found on pages 95, 98, 103–05, 110, 112 and 115.

For detailed information about population in each townland on the estate see Appendix 3.

Index